PE

mechanical
engineering

machine design
and materials

practice exam

Copyright ©2016 by NCEES®. All rights reserved.

All NCEES sample questions and solutions are copyrighted under the laws of the United States. No part of this publication may be reproduced, stored in a retrieval system, or transmitted in any form or by any means without the prior written permission of NCEES. Requests for permissions should be addressed in writing to permissions@ncees.org or to NCEES Exam Publications, PO Box 1686, Clemson, SC 29633.

ISBN 978-1-932613-77-3

Printed in the United States of America
1st printing November 2016

CONTENTS

Introduction to NCEES Exams 1
About NCEES
Updates on exam content and procedures
Exam-day schedule
Examinee Guide
Scoring and reporting
Staying connected

Exam Specifications 3

AM Practice Exam 7
PM Practice Exam 39

AM Solutions 67
PM Solutions 89

About NCEES
The National Council of Examiners for Engineering and Surveying (NCEES) is a nonprofit organization made up of engineering and surveying licensing boards from all U.S. states and territories. Since its founding in 1920, NCEES has been committed to advancing licensure for engineers and surveyors in order to protect the health, safety, and welfare of the American public.

NCEES helps its member licensing boards carry out their duties to regulate the professions of engineering and surveying. It develops best-practice models for state licensure laws and regulations and promotes uniformity among the states. It develops and administers the exams used for engineering and surveying licensure throughout the country. It also provides services to help licensed engineers and surveyors practice their professions in other U.S. states and territories.

Updates on exam content and procedures
Visit us at **ncees.org/exams** for updates on everything exam-related, including specifications, exam-day policies, scoring, and corrections to published exam preparation materials. This is also where you will register for the exam and find additional steps you should follow in your state to be approved for the exam.

Exam-day schedule
Be sure to arrive at the exam site on time. Late-arriving examinees will not be allowed into the exam room once the proctor has begun to read the exam script. The report time for the exam will be printed on your Exam Authorization. Normally, you will be given 1 hour between morning and afternoon sessions.

Examinee Guide
The *NCEES Examinee Guide* is the official guide to policies and procedures for all NCEES exams. All examinees are required to read this document before starting the exam registration process. You can download it at ncees.org/exams. It is your responsibility to make sure that you have the current version.

NCEES exams are administered in either a computer-based format or a pencil-and-paper format. Each method of administration has specific rules. This guide describes the rules for each exam format. Refer to the appropriate section for your exam.

Scoring and reporting
NCEES typically releases exam results to its member licensing boards 8–10 weeks after the exam. Depending on your state, you will be notified of your exam result online through your MyNCEES account or via mail from your state licensing board. Detailed information on the scoring process can be found at ncees.org/exams.

Staying connected
To keep up to date with NCEES announcements, events, and activities, connect with us on your preferred social media network.

EXAM SPECIFICATIONS

Principles and Practice of Engineering Examination
MECHANICAL—MACHINE DESIGN AND MATERIALS Exam Specifications
Effective Beginning with the April 2017 Examinations

- The exam is an 8-hour open-book exam. It contains 40 multiple-choice questions in the 4-hour morning session, and 40 multiple-choice questions in the 4-hour afternoon session. Examinee works all questions.

- The exam uses both the International System of units (SI) and the U.S. Customary System (USCS).

- The exam is developed with questions that will require a variety of approaches and methodologies, including design, analysis, and application.

- The knowledge areas specified as examples of kinds of knowledge are not exclusive or exhaustive categories.

	Approximate Number of Questions
I. Principles	**40**
A. Basic Engineering Practice	9
1. Engineering terms, symbols	
2. Interpretation of technical drawings	
3. Quality assurance/quality control (QA/QC)	
4. Project management and economic analysis	
5. Units and conversions	
6. Design methodology (e.g., identifying requirements, risk assessment, verification/validation)	
B. Engineering Science and Mechanics	10
1. Statics	
2. Kinematics	
3. Dynamics	
C. Material Properties	8
1. Physical (e.g., density, melting point, optical)	
2. Chemical (e.g., corrosion, alloys, oxidation)	
3. Mechanical	
a. Time-independent behavior (e.g., modulus, hardness, thermal expansion)	
b. Time-dependent behavior (e.g., creep, viscoelastic, thermal conductivity)	
D. Strength of Materials	10
1. Stress/strain (e.g., tension, compression)	
2. Shear	
3. Bending	
4. Buckling	
5. Torsion	

      6. Fatigue
      7. Failure theories (e.g., Von Mises, maximum shear stress)
  E. Vibration   3
      1. Natural frequencies (e.g., linear, bending, torsional) and acoustics
      2. Damping (e.g., frequency, damping ratio, critical damping)
      3. Forced vibrations (e.g., magnification factor, transmissibility, balancing, isolation)

II. Applications   40

  A. Mechanical Components   18
      1. Pressure vessels and piping (e.g., thick/thin wall)
      2. Bearings (e.g., types, lubrication analysis, life-load analysis)
      3. Gears (e.g., types, speed analysis, force analysis)
      4. Springs (e.g., types, force analysis, fatigue analysis)
      5. Dampers (e.g., types, selection)
      6. Belt, pulley and chain drives (e.g., types, force analysis)
      7. Clutches and brakes (e.g., types, torque/force analysis)
      8. Power screws (e.g., types, lifting and lowering torque, locking conditions)
      9. Shafts and keys (e.g., torsion, bending, static/fatigue failure, stress risers)
      10. Mechanisms (e.g., linkages, cams, slider crank, levers, force analysis, kinetic analysis)
      11. Basic mechatronics (e.g., electromechanical interfaces, sensors, basic circuits, basic controls)
      12. Hydraulic and pneumatic components (e.g., pumps, cylinders, presses)
      13. Motors and engines (e.g., energy conservation, efficiency)
  B. Joints and Fasteners   12
      1. Welding and brazing (e.g., types, symbols, stress analysis)
      2. Bolts, screws, rivets (e.g., grade/class selection, preload, fastener group force analysis)
      3. Adhesives (e.g., types, analysis)
  C. Supportive Knowledge   10
      1. Manufacturing processes (e.g., machining, molding, heat treatment)
      2. Fits and tolerances
      3. Codes and standards
      4. Computational methods and their limitations (e.g., FEA, CAE)
      5. Testing and instrumentation

AM PRACTICE EXAM

101. Which of the following symbols is commonly associated with tolerance of position in geometric dimensioning and tolerancing (e.g., in the ASME Y14.5 standard)?

(A) ⌀

(B) ▱

(C) ⌖

(D) ∠↗

102. A hydraulic cylinder is made up of a tube section with two ends and is held together by four tie rods as shown in the figure. The piston rod end is pressurized. Which data from the list below are necessary and sufficient to determine the shear stress in the threads at the piston rod to piston attachment?

(A) a, c, d, g, i
(B) c, d, e, h
(C) b, f, h, d
(D) a, d, e, h, i

a. Diameter of cylinder, d_{cyl} — 4.0 in.
b. Wall thickness of cylinder, t_{wall} — 0.25 in.
c. Length of cylinder, l — 12.0 in.
d. Piston thickness, T_{piston} — 2.0 in.
e. Piston rod diameter, d_{rod} — 1.5 in.
f. Thickness of rod end, $t_{rod\,end}$ — 3.0 in.
g. Tie rod diameter, d_{TR} — 0.75 in.
h. Fluid pressure, P — 2,500 psi
i. Piston-rod thread — 1–8 UNC

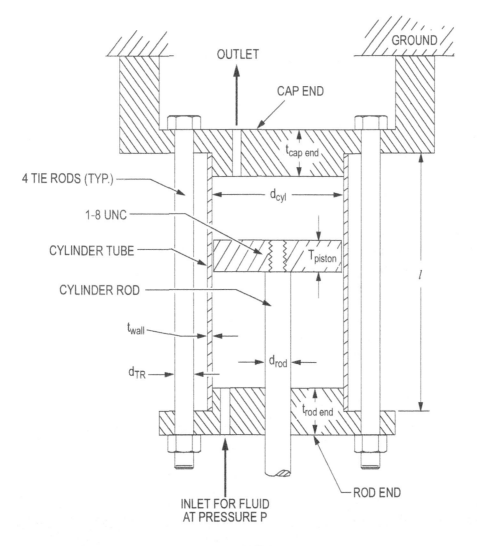

NOT TO SCALE

103. Table 1 shows the means for each subgroup from a measurement process over a 12-hr period. Each subgroup is made up of a sample size of 4.

TABLE 1

Subgroup	6:00 a.m.	9:00 a.m.	12:00 p.m.	3:00 p.m.	6:00 p.m.
1	7.30	7.70	8.40	8.70	6.70
2	7.00	7.20	7.50	8.20	7.30
3	6.80	7.50	7.80	7.90	7.10
4	7.10	7.90	8.20	8.50	7.30
5	7.20	7.90	8.70	8.50	6.90

Table 2 is an abbreviated list of the anti-biasing statistical constants.

TABLE 2

Sample Size	A_2	D_4	D_3
2	1.88	3.27	0.00
3	1.02	2.57	0.00
4	0.73	2.28	0.00
5	0.58	2.11	0.00
6	0.48	2.00	0.00

From the data provided in **Tables 1** and **2**, the upper control limit (UCL) and the lower control limit (LCL) of the process range (an R chart) are most nearly:

	UCL	LCL
(A)	3.42	0
(B)	1.09	−1.09
(C)	3.42	−3.42
(D)	17.0	0

MACHINE DESIGN AND MATERIALS AM PRACTICE EXAM

104. A manufacturing production department operates 80 hr/week. The process has a production rate of 60 units/hr, with a scrap rate of 1 out of 20 units. With a 10% lost production time allowance, the number of good units that can be made per week is most nearly:

(A) 4,100
(B) 4,300
(C) 4,500
(D) 4,800

105. A project consists of assembling a system using parts from Source X and Source Y.

Task	Description	Follows Task	Duration (days)
A	Acquire parts from Source X	None	2
B	Acquire parts from Source Y	A	2
C	Inspect parts	B	7
D	Test parts from Source X	A	11
E	Assemble parts and complete project	C and D	2

If the delivery of parts from Source X is delayed by 3 days, the total completion delay (days) will be most nearly:

(A) 0
(B) 1
(C) 2
(D) 3

MACHINE DESIGN AND MATERIALS AM PRACTICE EXAM

106. A manufacturing production department makes a family of similar parts. Part material cost is $12 for each part scrapped.

Machine	Labor Cost (per hour)	Production Rate (units per hour)	Part Scrap Rate	Part Setup Cost
1. Manual	$20	10	1 out of 32	$10
2. CNC* with manual load	$18	12	1 out of 80	$5
3. CNC* with auto load	$15	15	1 out of 60	$15
4. Dedicated automation	$12	60	1 out of 120	$250

*CNC–Computer Numerically Controlled Machine

The number of good parts per 80-hr workweek that can be made on the CNC with manual load (Machine No. 2) is most nearly:

(A) 600
(B) 948
(C) 960
(D) 1,180

107. Fracture toughness of a material is measured in units of $ksi\sqrt{in.}$ in the English system of units. A material with a fracture toughness of $35\ ksi\sqrt{in.}$ will have a fracture toughness in units of $MPa\sqrt{m}$ that is most nearly:

(A) 1
(B) 6
(C) 32
(D) 38

MACHINE DESIGN AND MATERIALS AM PRACTICE EXAM

108. An initial analysis of the critical speed of the cylindrical, steel lead screw for a proposed linear positioning system is to be performed using the equation given below.

$$\text{Critical speed} = \frac{215}{L^2}\sqrt{\frac{gEI}{\rho A}}$$

where:

- L = Length of lead screw
- E = modulus of elasticity
- I = area moment of inertia
- ρ = density
- A = cross-sectional area

Other Data:

Length of lead screw	48 in.
Root diameter of lead screw	0.84 in.
Young's modulus of steel	30,000,000 psi
Density of steel	490 lb/ft³

The critical speed (rpm) of the lead screw is most nearly:

(A) 1,150
(B) 3,950
(C) 91,250
(D) 190,000

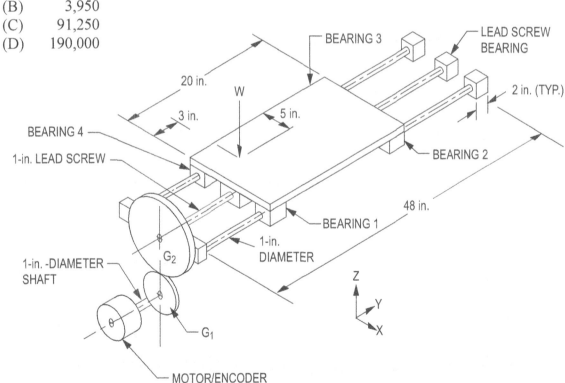

NOT TO SCALE

MACHINE DESIGN AND MATERIALS AM PRACTICE EXAM

109. Which of the following lists could be a structural decomposition of the design for an automobile?

(A) Quiet
Distinctive
Rapid acceleration
Sleek profile
Reliable
Energy efficient

(B) Engine
Wheels
Frame
Seats
Axles
Body

(C) Protect passengers
Transport passengers
Transport cargo
Provide prestige to passengers

(D) Start engine
Accelerate
Decelerate
Steer
Load cargo
Transport cargo

MACHINE DESIGN AND MATERIALS AM PRACTICE EXAM

110. Which of the following iron-carbon alloys consists of nearly equal amounts of pearlite and ferrite when cooled at a slow rate from 1,800°F to room temperature?

(A) Class 40 grey cast iron
(B) AISI 304
(C) AISI 1040
(D) AISI 1095

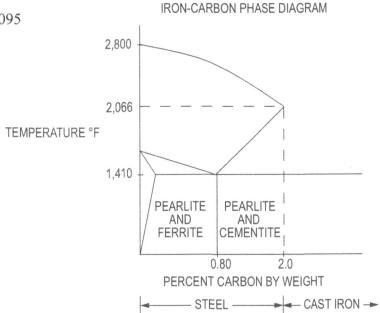

MACHINE DESIGN AND MATERIALS AM PRACTICE EXAM

111. A circular rod will be loaded in simple tension. The rod has a length of 10 in. and a radius 3/8 in. Data for available materials are as follows:

Material	Yield Strength (psi)	Weight (lb/in³)	Cost ($/lb)
Steel	48,000	0.3	0.15
Aluminum	40,000	0.1	0.82
Titanium	175,000	0.2	2.72
Magnesium	22,000	0.06	0.91

Which rod material should be selected to give the highest strength-to-weight ratio while meeting the requirement of costing less than $0.08?

(A) Steel

(B) Aluminum

(C) Titanium

(D) Magnesium

112. A steel ($E = 30 \times 10^6$ psi) bar having a cross-sectional area of 0.375 in^2 is mounted as shown in the figure. The spring has a spring constant of 10,000 lb/in. If the nominal coefficient of thermal expansion is 6×10^{-6} in./(in.-°F), the increase in force (lb) produced in the bar by a temperature increase of 300°F is most nearly:

(A) 24
(B) 324
(C) 624
(D) 724

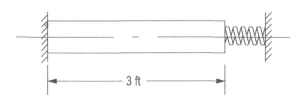

113. The figure shown is representative of the stress-strain relationship of:

   I. Aluminum alloys
   II. Cast iron
   III. Copper alloys
   IV. Mild steels

(A) I only

(B) I, III

(C) II, IV

(D) IV only

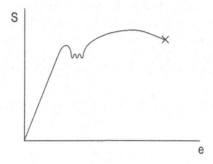

MACHINE DESIGN AND MATERIALS AM PRACTICE EXAM

114. Four steel rods, each with a cross-sectional area of 1 in², are embedded in a 5-in.-diameter light aggregate concrete cylinder. The steel has a yield strength of 36,000 psi and a modulus of elasticity of 30×10^6 psi. The concrete has a compressive strength of 3,100 psi and a modulus of elasticity of 3×10^6 psi. A rigid plate is placed over both ends of the cylinder, and a compressive axial force of 100,000 lb is applied. The stress (psi) induced in the steel rods is most nearly:

(A) 1,800
(B) 5,100
(C) 18,000
(D) 25,000

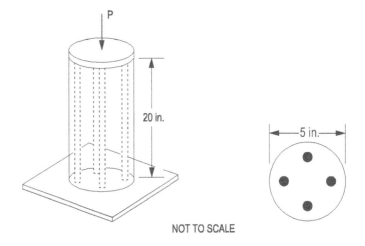

115. A 2-in. copper pipe is to be connected to a 2-in. black steel pipe. Based on corrosion considerations, which of the following is the best connection choice?

(A) Threaded coupling
(B) MIG welding
(C) Pipe brazing
(D) Dielectric union

MACHINE DESIGN AND MATERIALS AM PRACTICE EXAM

116. A piece of steel has a Rockwell C hardness of 28.8. The tensile strength (psi) of the steel is most nearly:

(A) 152,000
(B) 139,000
(C) 54,000
(D) 15,000

117. A 2-in. × 2-in. steel bar is installed as shown. The steel has a temperature coefficient of expansion $\alpha = 6 \times 10^{-6}$ in./(in.-°F) and $E = 30 \times 10^6$ psi. The normal operating temperature is 76°F. The temperature is increased by 250°F. The steel bar has no preload and is set between two rigid walls. The engineering stress (psi) in the steel bar at the new temperature is most nearly:

(A) 59,000
(B) 45,000
(C) 31,000
(D) 24,000

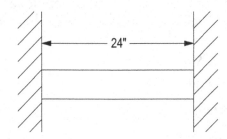

MACHINE DESIGN AND MATERIALS AM PRACTICE EXAM

118. A linear spring-mass system consisting of a spring with a spring constant of 20 lbf/in. and a mass of 10 lbm undergoes free vibration. The linear frequency (cycles/sec) of this vibration is most nearly:

(A) 0.78
(B) 1.3
(C) 4.4
(D) 28

119. For a system described by the equation $X_t = 2.2e^{-2.2t} \sin(2.2t + 0.384)$, the damped time period (sec) is most nearly:

(A) 2.85
(B) 4.75
(C) 6.33
(D) 8.86

120. A machine with a 24-in.-diameter rotating drum has vibration isolation mounts that provide damping at half of the critical damping value. Unknown to anyone during installation, a bolt was left inside the machine and, due to frictional forces, acts as if it were attached to the wall of the rotating drum. The maximum displacement amplitude of the steady-state response occurs at a frequency (as a percentage of the natural frequency of the system) that is most nearly:

(A) 71%
(B) 100%
(C) 141%
(D) 200%

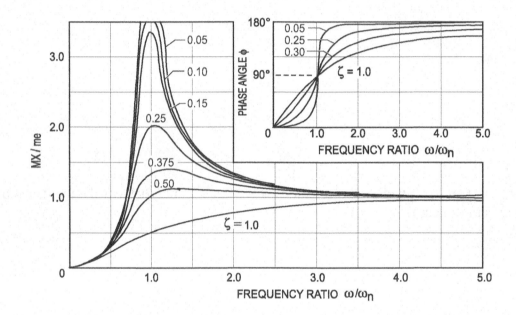

MACHINE DESIGN AND MATERIALS AM PRACTICE EXAM

121. For the bracket shown in the figure, the allowable shear stress in the weld is 12,000 psi. Ignore any allowance for starting and stopping of weld. Neglecting the vertical shear stress, the minimum size (in.) of weld required to resist the torsional shear stress is most nearly:

(A) 1/4
(B) 3/8
(C) 5/8
(D) 3/4

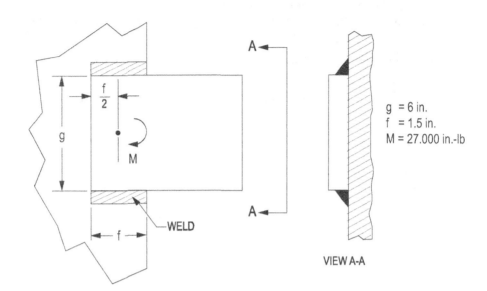

$g = 6$ in.
$f = 1.5$ in.
$M = 27{,}000$ in.-lb

VIEW A-A

122. A machining operation creates a hole for a 3/8-16NC × 0.75-in.-long countersink head screw, as shown in **Figure 1**. A cutter is used to create the countersink recess as shown in **Figure 2**. The process steps are as follows:

1. Drill through with a tap drill diameter of 5/16 in.
2. Countersink the tap drill hole to a depth of Dimension A, so that the screw head will be flush with the part surface.
3. Tap the hole 3/8-16NC.

To complete Step 2, the depth (in.) of Dimension A is most nearly:

(A) 0.202
(B) 0.234
(C) 0.269
(D) 0.313

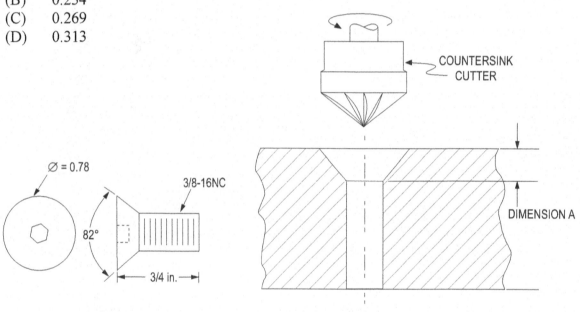

FIGURE 1   **FIGURE 2**

MACHINE DESIGN AND MATERIALS AM PRACTICE EXAM

123. The 2,500-lbf load shown in the figure is supported by a beam that is secured by six 3/4-in.-diameter bolts in a hexagonal array with neighboring bolts 3 in. apart. The shear stress is greatest in which bolt?

(A) 1
(B) 2
(C) 3
(D) 4

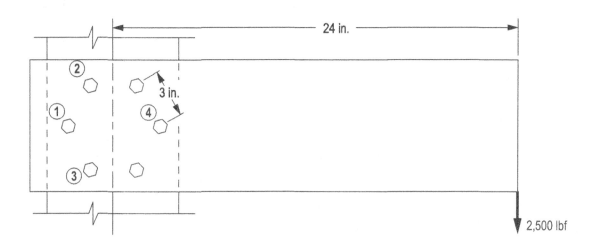

MACHINE DESIGN AND MATERIALS AM PRACTICE EXAM

124. A blind pressure vessel flange is restrained by eight equally spaced 1/2-in.–13 UNC steel bolts. To maintain an adequate seal, each bolt is preloaded to 5,000 lb. The bolt stiffness k_b and the material stiffness k_m are numerically equal. The bolt stress (psi) for an internal pressure of 500 psi is most nearly:

(A) 10,000
(B) 50,000
(C) 60,000
(D) 85,000

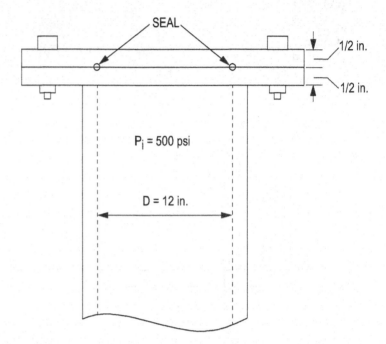

MACHINE DESIGN AND MATERIALS AM PRACTICE EXAM

125. A 1/2-in. steel plate is attached to a vertical structural steel channel with three 1/2-in.–13 UNC bolts, as shown. The load (lb) that the highest loaded bolt will carry is most nearly:

(A) 167
(B) 625
(C) 792
(D) 960

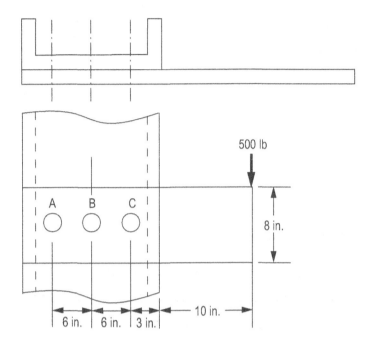

MACHINE DESIGN AND MATERIALS AM PRACTICE EXAM

126. The ratio of tensile strengths of a 1/2-in. SAE Grade 8 bolt to a 1/2-in. SAE Grade 2 bolt is most nearly:

    (A)   2
    (B)   3
    (C)   4
    (D)   5

127. A joint is modified to include a longer bolt and a steel spacer (Part A) as shown in the figure. One of the consequences of this change is to:

    (A)   increase the effective bolt stiffness

    (B)   increase the impact capability of the joint

    (C)   increase joint preload

    (D)   decrease joint compression

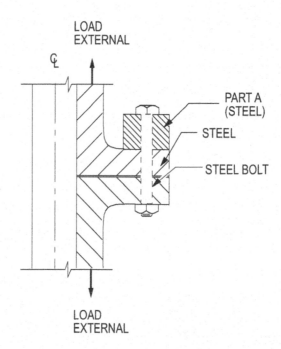

MACHINE DESIGN AND MATERIALS AM PRACTICE EXAM

128. A 30-in.-long laminate beam is made by gluing together three 1-in. × 1-in. × 30-in. pieces (full size) with a cross section as shown. If this is used in an application where the vertical shear is 1,000 lb, the shear stress (psi) in the adhesive would be most nearly:

(A) 670
(B) 440
(C) 220
(D) 110

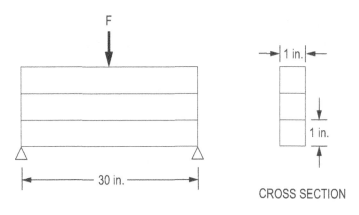

129. Which symbol properly indicates a field bevel-groove weld?

(A)

(B)

(C)

(D)

130. A hanger bracket is shown. The hanger must support a vertical load of 19,600 lb (as indicated in the figure) with a factor of safety of 4. The hanger will be welded with an E-6010 rod that has a shear yield strength of 24,000 lb/in². The size (in.) of the fillet weld that is required is most nearly:

(A) 1/8
(B) 1/4
(C) 3/8
(D) 1/2

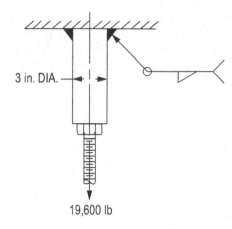

131. A hanger bracket is made up of a weldment and a 1 1/4–7 Grade 5 threaded rod. Based on yield strengths of the rod and using a factor of safety of 4, the load (lbf) the rod can support is most nearly:

(A) 78,500
(B) 22,300
(C) 21,700
(D) 19,600

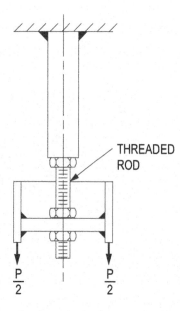

MACHINE DESIGN AND MATERIALS AM PRACTICE EXAM

132. Three plates are bonded with epoxy in a double-lap joint as shown. The shear strength of the epoxy is 1,500 psi. Assuming the epoxy coverage is 80%, the maximum pulling force P (lb) that the bond can withstand is most nearly:

(A) 4,800
(B) 6,000
(C) 9,600
(D) 12,000

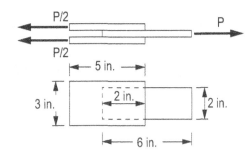

133. A process requires 5,000 lb/hr of plastic [C_p = 0.5 Btu/(lb-°F)] to be cooled from 600°F to 400°F in a counterflow heat exchanger with a 70% efficiency. The secondary coolant is water [C_p = 1.0 Btu/(lb-°F)] entering the heat exchanger at 55°F and leaving at 90°F. The water (ρ_v = 8.3 lb/gal) flow (gpm) required for cooling is most nearly:

(A) 20
(B) 29
(C) 41
(D) 340

MACHINE DESIGN AND MATERIALS AM PRACTICE EXAM

134. Referring to the figure, the minimum material thickness (mm) between Holes A and B is most nearly:

(A) 0.2
(B) 0.3
(C) 0.4
(D) 0.5

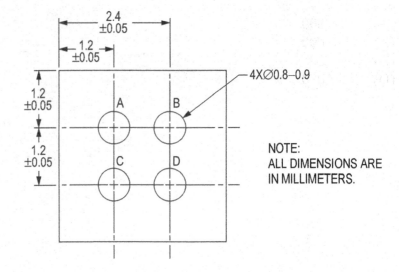

NOTE: ALL DIMENSIONS ARE IN MILLIMETERS.

135. A 42-tooth pinion running at 1,800 rpm drives a gear at 1,080 rpm. The spur gear pair is to be enclosed in a cylindrical casing with a total diametral clearance of 1/2 in. The diametral pitch is 6 teeth/in. The **minimum** required casing diameter (in.) is most nearly:

(A) 12.0
(B) 19.0
(C) 19.2
(D) 19.5

MACHINE DESIGN AND MATERIALS AM PRACTICE EXAM

136. A wedge-testing fixture must be designed to test an ANSI B18.2.1 standard hex bolt with 5/8-11-UNC threads per ASTM F606 3.5.1, shown below. In specifying the outer diameter of the wedge D, the diameter of the hole in the wedge d, the radius of the hole R, and the wedge thickness T, all in inches, which of the following sets of dimensions most closely satisfies the test standard?

	D	**d**	**R**	**T**
(A)	0.95	0.675	0.030	0.313
(B)	1.25	0.675	0.060	0.313
(C)	1.20	0.692	0.030	0.313
(D)	1.20	0.692	0.060	0.625

The following is an excerpt from ASTM F606:

3.5.1　The wedge shall have a thickness at the thin side of the hole equal to one half the nominal diameter of the bolt. The hole in the wedge shall have a clearance over the nominal size of the bolt and its edges top and bottom shall be rounded as specified in Table 3. The minimum outside dimension of the wedge should be such that at no time during the test should any corner loading of the head of the product (adjacent to the wedge) occur.

Table 2. American National Standard and Unified Standard Hex and Heavy Hex Bolts
(ANSI B18.2.1-1981, R1992)

Nominal Size or Basic Diam.	Body Diam. E Max.	Width Across Flats F			Width Across Corners G		Height H			Thread Length L_T Basic
		Basic	Max.	Min.	Max.	Min.	Basic	Max.	Min.	
HEX BOLTS										
1/4	0.2500	0.260	7/16	0.438	0.425	0.505	0.484	11/64	0.188	0.150	0.750
5/16	0.3125	0.324	1/2	0.500	0.484	0.577	0.552	7/32	0.235	0.195	0.875
3/8	0.3750	0.388	9/16	0.562	0.544	0.650	0.620	1/4	0.268	0.226	1.000
7/16	0.4375	0.452	5/8	0.625	0.603	0.722	0.687	19/64	0.316	0.272	1.125
1/2	0.5000	0.515	3/4	0.750	0.725	0.866	0.826	11/32	0.364	0.302	1.250
5/8	0.6250	0.642	15/16	0.938	0.906	1.083	1.033	27/64	0.444	0.378	1.500
3/4	0.7500	0.768	1 1/8	1.125	1.088	1.299	1.240	1/2	0.524	0.455	1.750
7/8	0.8750	0.895	1 5/16| 1.312	1.269	1.516	1.447	37/64	0.604	0.531	2.000
	1.0000	1.022	1 1/2	1.500	1.450	1.732	1.653	43/64	0.700	0.591	2.250

Table 3. Tensile Wedge Test Hole Clearance Details

Nominal Product Size (in.)	Nominal Clearance in Hole (in.)	Nominal Radius on Corners of Hole (in.)
1/4–1/2	0.030	0.030
9/16–3/4	0.050	0.060
7/8–1	0.060	0.060

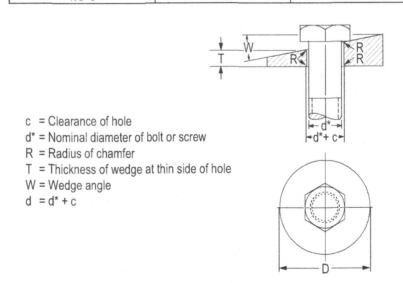

c = Clearance of hole
d* = Nominal diameter of bolt or screw
R = Radius of chamfer
T = Thickness of wedge at thin side of hole
W = Wedge angle
d = d* + c

137. As shown in the figure, a block with two pins of given size tolerance must mate with a block with two holes of given size tolerance. The smallest hole diameter D (in.) that will allow the parts to mate is most nearly:

(A) 0.240
(B) 0.260
(C) 0.290
(D) 0.320

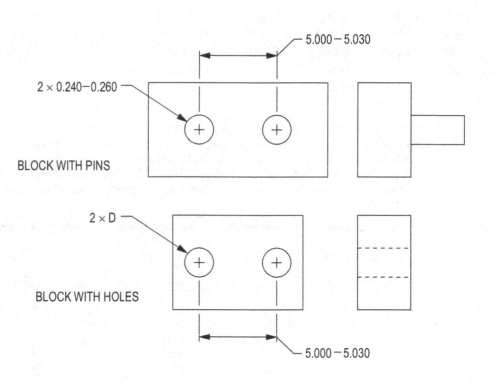

NOT TO SCALE

MACHINE DESIGN AND MATERIALS AM PRACTICE EXAM

138. A steel beam manufacturer wants to use a strain gage to measure the maximum load that a steel beam can support prior to buckling. A standard procedure to perform the measurement is most likely to be found in a publication by which of the following organizations?

(A) ASTM

(B) Underwriters' Laboratory (UL©)

(C) ASME

(D) SAE

139. Four axial strain gages configured in a full Wheatstone bridge circuit are used for validation testing on a circular beam loaded in torsion. Which of the following is the most appropriate layout for the gages?

(A)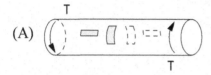

(B)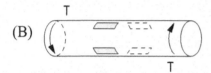

(C)

(D)

MACHINE DESIGN AND MATERIALS AM PRACTICE EXAM

140. A class FN2 fit is desired between a steel shaft with a nominal diameter of 1.50 in. and a cast iron hub. Using the table provided, the minimum diameter (in.) of the shaft is:

(A) 1.5000
(B) 1.5018
(C) 1.5024
(D) 1.6800

ANSI Standard Force and Shrink Fits

Nominal Size Range, Inches Over To	Class FN 2		
	Interference	Standard Tolerance Limits	
		Hole H7	Shaft s6
	Values shown below are in thousandths of an inch		
0– 0.12	0.2 0.85	+0.4 0	+0.85 +0.6
0.12– 0.24	0.2 1.0	+0.5 0	+1.0 +0.7
0.24– 0.40	0.4 1.4	+0.6 0	+1.4 +1.0
0.40– 0.56	0.5 1.6	+0.7 0	+1.6 +1.2
0.56– 0.71	0.5 1.6	+0.7 0	+1.6 +1.2
0.71– 0.95	0.6 1.9	+0.8 0	+1.9 +1.4
0.95– 1.19	0.6 1.9	+0.8 0	+1.9 +1.4
1.19– 1.58	0.8 2.4	+1.0 0	+2.4 +1.8
1.58– 1.97	0.8 2.4	+1.0 0	+2.4 +1.8
1.97– 2.56	0.8 2.7	+1.2 0	+2.7 +2.0
2.56– 3.15	1.0 2.9	+1.2 0	+2.9 +2.2
3.15– 3.94	1.4 3.7	+1.4 0	+3.7 +2.8
3.94– 4.73	1.6 3.9	+1.4 0	+3.9 +3.0
4.73– 5.52	1.9 4.5	+1.6 0	+4.5 +3.5

Adapted from ASME B4.1-1981 (R2009), American Society of Mechanical Engineers. All rights reserved.

This completes the morning session.
Solutions begin on page 67.

PM PRACTICE EXAM

MACHINE DESIGN AND MATERIALS PM PRACTICE EXAM

501. A cord is wrapped halfway around a 2-in.-O.D. pipe as shown. The coefficient of friction (dynamic and static) between the cord and pipe is $\mu = 0.35$. A box with a weight of 50 lb is suspended from one end of the cord and a force P applied to the other end. The minimum force P (lb) required to raise the 50-lb box is most nearly:

(A) 16.7
(B) 50.0
(C) 85.0
(D) 150.0

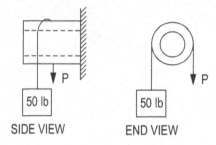

502. A ladder leaning against a wall slides down and, when it is in the position shown, the magnitudes of the velocities of the endpoints A and B are $V_A = 3$ m/s and $V_B = 4$ m/s. The magnitude of the velocity (m/s) of the midpoint C is most nearly:

(A) 5.0
(B) 4.0
(C) 3.5
(D) 2.5

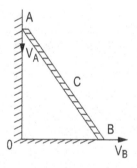

MACHINE DESIGN AND MATERIALS PM PRACTICE EXAM

503. A turbo pump impeller disk weighing 41.0 lb is mounted in the middle of a shaft. The shaft is supported by single-row ball bearings spaced 18.0 in. apart. All materials are 440C, stainless steel ($E = 28.6 \times 10^6$ psi). For a shaft diameter of 1.18 in. (neglect the weight of the shaft), the critical speed (rpm) would be most nearly:

(A) 460
(B) 920
(C) 4,400
(D) 8,790

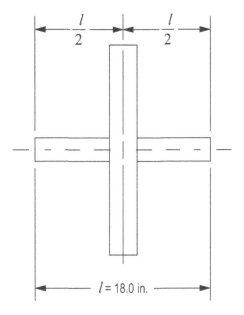

Copyright 2016 by NCEES

MACHINE DESIGN AND MATERIALS PM PRACTICE EXAM

504. A bracket is constructed using two tubes and a solid plate as shown in the figure. Assume each tube is rigidly attached to the plate and fixed against bending and twisting on the other end. The dimensions are as follows:

a = 900 mm
b = 600 mm
c = 250 mm

Which dimensions are necessary and sufficient to determine the reaction at the end of each tube?

(A) a, b only
(B) a, b, c
(C) b only
(D) b, c only

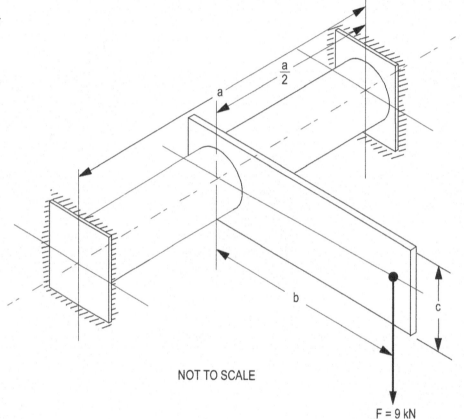

NOT TO SCALE

F = 9 kN

MACHINE DESIGN AND MATERIALS PM PRACTICE EXAM

505. A passenger car has the following specifications:

    Rear wheel drive
    Vehicle weight   2,400 lbm
    Vehicle wheelbase, front to rear   100 in.
    Static weight distribution   25% at each wheel location
    Center of gravity   18 in. above ground, centered over wheelbase

Assume this vehicle, moving at a constant velocity, has a driving force of 400 lbf at each rear wheel. Neglect suspension effects and rolling resistance, and assume the drag force acts on the center of gravity. The normal force (lbf) on each rear wheel is most nearly:

(A)   316
(B)   576
(C)   672
(D)   1,130

506. The device shown is used to determine the static coefficient of friction between two materials. A block made of the first material is placed on a plank made of the second material, which is initially horizontal as shown in the figure. The plank is then raised as shown. When h = 5 in., the block starts to slide. For these conditions, the coefficient of static friction is most nearly:

(A)   0.42
(B)   0.46
(C)   0.50
(D)   0.58

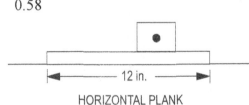
HORIZONTAL PLANK

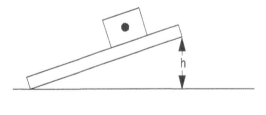
RAISED PLANK

507. A car traveling at 65 mph must be able to stop within a distance of 400 ft. The wheel diameter is 28 in. Assume no brakes lock up during this braking; all brakes are on for total time duration. Neglect rolling resistance and aerodynamic drag.

The angular deceleration (rad/s^2) of the wheel as the car brakes uniformly from 65 mph to a stop over a distance of 400 ft is most nearly:

(A) 4.7
(B) 6.5
(C) 9.7
(D) 15.7

508. A projectile is launched at an angle of 40° toward a suspended target as shown. The initial launch velocity (ft/sec) required for the projectile to strike the target while at the peak of its trajectory is most nearly:

(A) 80
(B) 105
(C) 108
(D) 125

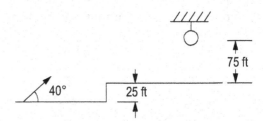

MACHINE DESIGN AND MATERIALS PM PRACTICE EXAM

509. A bullet weighing 3.24 g and traveling at 610 m/s strikes a 567-g wooden block hanging from a string. The distance from the attachment to the center of mass of the block is 2.00 m. If the bullet fully embeds into the block, and ignoring any rotation of the block, the maximum lateral displacement D (m) of the bullet-block system is most nearly:

(A) 0.612
(B) 0.844
(C) 1.44
(D) 1.90

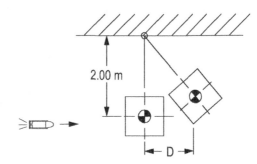

510. A device for lifting a block weighing 400 lb is shown. Ignoring the weight of the lifting device, the minimum coefficient of friction required to hold the block is most nearly:

(A) 0.23
(B) 0.39
(C) 0.78
(D) 0.95

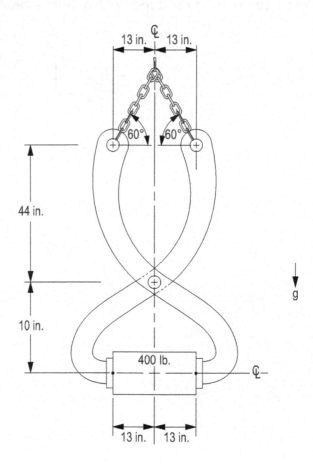

511. Assuming a factor of safety of 2.5 and neglecting the weight of the beam, the maximum load P (lb) that can be supported by the beam shown is most nearly:

(A) 3,550
(B) 8,875
(C) 22,188
(D) 42,600

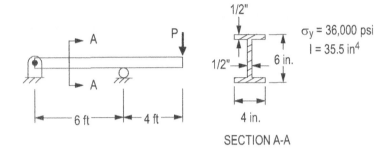

512. A 1/2-in.-diameter pipe hanger rod is loaded in tension with a 2,300-lb force. If the rod is 6 in. long and is made of a material with the stress-strain relationship shown, the total elongation (in.) it will experience is most nearly:

(A) 0.0004
(B) 0.002
(C) 0.005
(D) 0.01

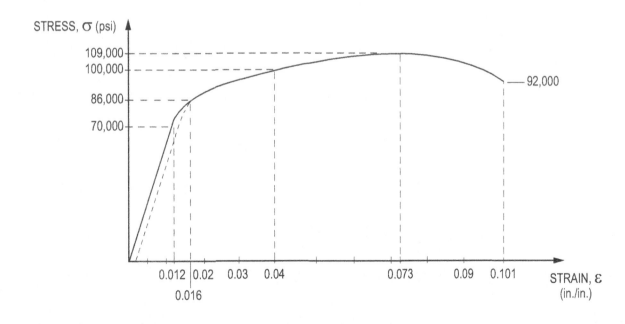

MACHINE DESIGN AND MATERIALS PM PRACTICE EXAM

513. A 24-in.-long cantilever beam carries a uniformly distributed load of 10 lb/in. over 12 in. as shown in the figure. The shear force (lb) in the beam at a distance of 18 in. from the wall is most nearly:

(A) 60
(B) 75
(C) 90
(D) 120

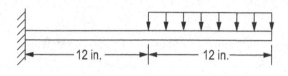

514. A beam is loaded as shown in the figure. The maximum bending moment (N·m) is most nearly:

(A) 1,000
(B) 800
(C) 700
(D) 600

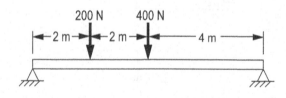

MACHINE DESIGN AND MATERIALS PM PRACTICE EXAM

515. A simply supported, uniformly loaded beam is found to deflect excessively when subjected to a fixed total load. Assume the beam is made of metal and has a rectangular cross section. If the length cannot be changed, the deflection can best be reduced by at least 50% by:

(A) selecting a different material having double the modulus of elasticity

(B) reducing the depth of the beam by 50%

(C) selecting a different material having double the yield strength

(D) selecting a different material having double the Poisson ratio

516. A machine element 2 m long with a cross section 100 mm × 250 mm is loaded in compression as shown in the top figure. It is made of a high-strength aluminum alloy (E = 70 GPa, σ_{yield} = 432 MPa). Assume ideal conditions. If the element is supported in all directions at the location shown in the bottom figure, the compression failure load will:

(A) increase by a factor of approximately 2

(B) increase by a factor of approximately 3

(C) increase by a factor of 4

(D) There is no change in the failure load.

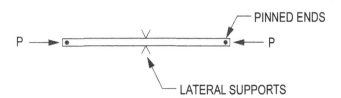

MACHINE DESIGN AND MATERIALS PM PRACTICE EXAM

517. Assuming a shear modulus of elasticity G = 90 GPa and modulus of elasticity E = 210 GPa, the torsional stiffness (N·m/rad) of the motor shaft shown in the figure is most nearly:

(A) 90×10^3

(B) 180×10^3

(C) 90×10^6

(D) 180×10^6

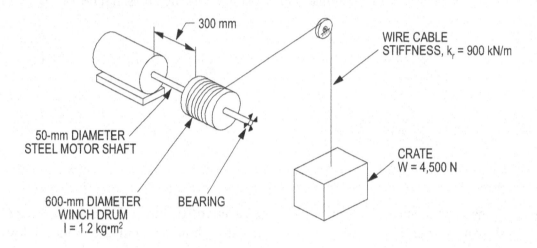

518. Fatigue test specimens made of a certain steel are subjected to completely reversed loading. At a stress amplitude of 90,000 psi, the life is 1,000 cycles. At 50,000 psi, the life is 1,000,000 cycles. The number of cycles expected before failure at a stress amplitude of 70,000 psi is most nearly:

(A) 20,000
(B) 100,000
(C) 500,000
(D) 1,000,000

519. In the Goodman diagram shown, where S_e is the fatigue limit, which point(s) represents a definite finite life?

(A) Point 2 only
(B) Points 2 and 5
(C) Point 4 only
(D) Point 5 only

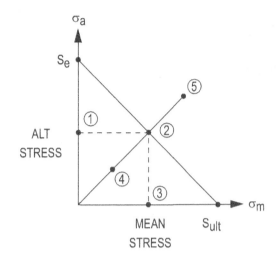

520. A cylindrical pressure vessel with hemispherical end caps is unrestrained. The diameter is 1 m, the wall thickness is 1 cm, and the internal gage pressure is 3 MPa. If the tensile yield strength S_{yt} is 450 MPa and the von Mises failure criterion is used, then the factor of safety ($S_{yt}/\sigma_{effective}$) is most nearly:

(A) 1.5
(B) 1.7
(C) 3.0
(D) 3.5

521. A hydraulic cylinder with an inside diameter of 24 in. is subjected to an internal pressure of 7,500 psi. Ignore end effects. Knowing the cylinder is not a thin-walled pressure vessel, and using an allowable stress of 20,000 psi, the required thickness (in.) is most nearly:

(A) 5.80
(B) 4.50
(C) 2.25
(D) 2.07

522. A single-row ball bearing is subjected to a radial load of 75 lb (with no axial load), has a rated life of 180,000 min, and a rated speed of 500 rpm. The allowable radial load (lb) of the bearing when rotating at 10 rad/sec with a design life of 268,000 min is most nearly:

(A) 264
(B) 114
(C) 90
(D) 66

MACHINE DESIGN AND MATERIALS PM PRACTICE EXAM

523. A passenger car has the following specifications:

Rear wheel drive	
Engine torque at crankshaft	500 N·m max
Transmission efficiency	0.90
Rear differential efficiency	0.80
Rear wheel diameter	750 mm
Rear differential pinion gear	16 teeth
Rear differential ring gear	52 teeth
Vehicle weight	12,000 N
Vehicle wheelbase	2.5 m
Static weight distribution	25% at each wheel location
Vehicle center of gravity height	500 mm
Tire-to-roadway max coefficient of friction	0.9 (for both longitudinal and lateral direction)
Transmission ratio	1:1

The rear differential ring gear is changed to 45 teeth. Which of the following statements is true?

(A) The vehicle acceleration will increase.

(B) The vehicle speed at a given engine rpm will increase.

(C) Both (A) and (B) are true.

(D) Both (A) and (B) are false.

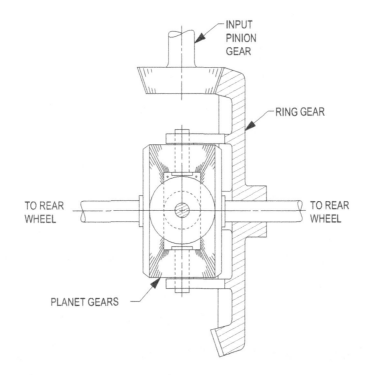

Copyright 2016 by NCEES

MACHINE DESIGN AND MATERIALS PM PRACTICE EXAM

524. A torsional spring is under a fluctuating torque that varies from +25 lb-in. to +50 lb-in. The torques (lb-in.) used to estimate the fatigue life are most nearly:

	T_a	T_m
(A)	12.5	37.5
(B)	50	25
(C)	25	25
(D)	25	50

MACHINE DESIGN AND MATERIALS PM PRACTICE EXAM

525. A commercial-grade, straight-bevel gear and pinion, both with an allowable bending stress of 70,000 psi, are shown in the figure. The shafts intersect at 90°. The tooth form is a full-depth involute with a pressure angle of 20°. The gear is operating at 10 hp. The following data apply:

	Pinion	Gear
Diametral pitch, P_d	6	6
No. of teeth	20	40
Operating speed	–	600 rpm
Geometry factor, J	0.21	0.21
Horsepower	–	10
Pitch angle, γ	26.56°	–

The magnitude of the thrust load (lb) on the pinion shaft is most nearly:

(A) 26
(B) 51
(C) 103
(D) 324

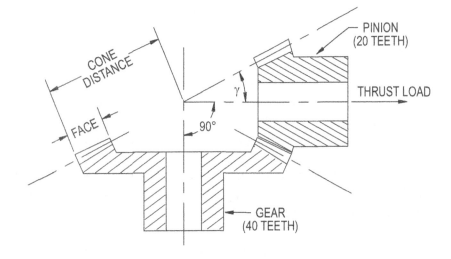

MACHINE DESIGN AND MATERIALS PM PRACTICE EXAM

526. Material compatibility concerns require that a steel spring made from wire with a shear modulus of 11×10^6 psi be redesigned. Brass with a shear modulus of 5.5×10^6 psi will be used instead. The steel wire has a diameter of 0.15 in. The spring diameter and the number of turns must be the same for the steel and brass springs. If the spring constant of the brass spring is to be the same as that of the steel spring, the diameter (in.) of the brass wire must be most nearly:

(A) 0.12
(B) 0.15
(C) 0.18
(D) 0.30

527. A spring is made from 0.1055-in.-diameter wire. If the spring has a free length of 3 in., a spring constant of 20 lb/in., and 10 total coils (ground and squared ends), the force (lb) required to fully compress the spring is most nearly:

(A) 14
(B) 32
(C) 39
(D) 71

MACHINE DESIGN AND MATERIALS PM PRACTICE EXAM

528. A belt pulley has a 42-in. diameter and rotates at 250 rpm. The 4-in.-wide belt has an angle of contact of 135° over the pulley. If the coefficient of friction between the pulley and the belt is 0.25 and the maximum tension in the belt is 80 lb/in. of width, the maximum horsepower that can be transmitted by the belt is most nearly:

(A) 12
(B) 65
(C) 141
(D) 178

529. A 40-mm-diameter shaft has a keyway that is 8 mm wide. The key is made of steel with a yield strength in tension of 200 MPa. In order to transmit 320 N·m of torque, the minimum key length (mm) required is most nearly:

(A) 5
(B) 8
(C) 10
(D) 20

MACHINE DESIGN AND MATERIALS PM PRACTICE EXAM

530. An initial analysis must be performed on the design of a proposed linear positioning system as shown in the figure. All components are steel unless otherwise noted.

Other Data:
    Size of table   20 in. × 16 in. × 1 in.
    No. of teeth on G_1 16
    No. of teeth on G_2 48
    Pitch of lead screw   0.125 in.
    Length of lead screw   48 in.
    E for steel   30,000,000 psi

If the 1-in.-diameter lead screw has a root diameter of 0.84 in., the axial stiffness (lb/in.) of the lead screw prior to the installation of the table is most nearly:

(A)   90,000
(B)   210,000
(C)   410,000
(D)   830,000

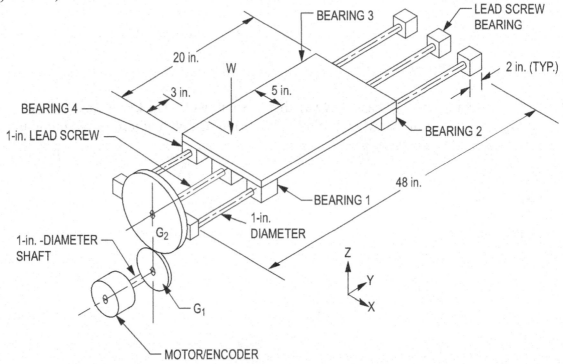

NOT TO SCALE

MACHINE DESIGN AND MATERIALS PM PRACTICE EXAM

531. The figure shows a schematic of a can-crushing device. The device consists of a slider at A that moves in a horizontal guide with an opening to discharge the crushed can. Pin joints connect Links AC and BD, and the slider at A. All links and the pins at A, B, and D are made with materials having the following physical properties:

Modulus of elasticity	30×10^6 psi
Yield strength, S_y	60,000 psi
Ultimate strength, S_u	100,000 psi
Shear strength	20,000 psi

Link BD, of length 7.07 in., is made out of a solid bar of circular cross section and is designed to carry an axial load of 500 lb. A safety factor of 2 against yield and 1.5 against buckling is desired for safety reasons. The diameter (in.) of the bar used for Link BD is most nearly:

(A) 0.103
(B) 0.146
(C) 0.184
(D) 0.225

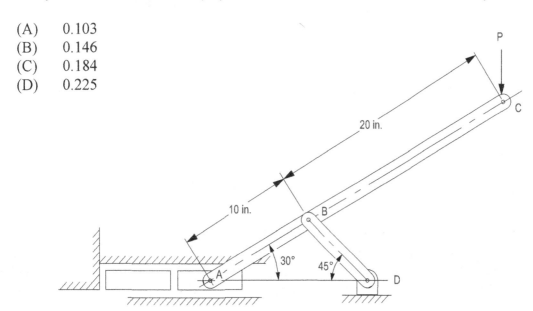

532. An electrical circuit is shown. The equivalent resistance of the loop is R_e. Which of the following statements is true?

(A) $V_1 + V_2 = IR_1 + IR_2$

(B) $\dfrac{V_1}{R_1 + R_2} = \dfrac{V_2}{R_3}$

(C) $R_e = R_1 + R_2 + R_3$

(D) $\dfrac{1}{R_1} + \dfrac{1}{R_2} = \dfrac{1}{R_3}$

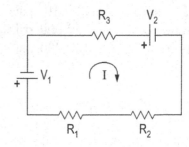

533. The hydraulic cylinder shown in the figure has a 2.75-in.-diameter piston (Area, A = 5.94 in^2) and is subjected to a maximum pressure of 3,000 psi. The effective column length of the high-strength rod is 50 in. when treated as having pinned ends. Using a safety factor of 2.0 with respect to buckling on a material having a yield strength of 36,500 psi and modulus of elasticity of 30×10^6 psi, the required rod diameter (in.) is most nearly:

(A) 1.11
(B) 1.32
(C) 1.57
(D) 2.22

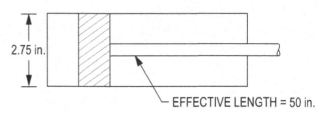

MACHINE DESIGN AND MATERIALS PM PRACTICE EXAM

534. A 230-V ac single-phase, 10-hp motor operates at 80% power factor and its rated load. If the efficiency of the motor is 65%, the current (amperes) drawn is most nearly:

(A) 12
(B) 17
(C) 40
(D) 62

535. A centrifugal pump operating at 1,750 rpm consumes 1,000 hp. If the speed of the pump is reduced to 1,000 rpm, the power consumption (kW) will be most nearly:

(A) 426
(B) 243
(C) 187
(D) 139

MACHINE DESIGN AND MATERIALS PM PRACTICE EXAM

536. A uniform thin disk with mass 10 kg is brought up to a speed of 50 rad/s and then disconnected from the driver. The disk is stopped by a brake as shown. If a force P of 150 N is applied to the brake, how long (sec) does it take the disk to stop?

(A) 0.19
(B) 0.38
(C) 0.42
(D) 0.77

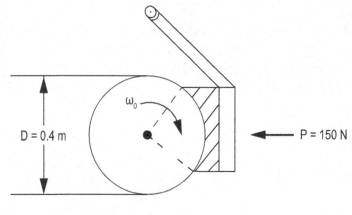

μ for brake pad = 0.8
Contact angle, Φ = 80°

MACHINE DESIGN AND MATERIALS PM PRACTICE EXAM

537. Torque T is applied to the power screw with collar as shown to raise or lower the load F. The power screw has a triple-start square thread. The torque T (lb-in.) required to raise a load F = 1,700 lb is most nearly:

(A) 383
(B) 308
(C) 242
(D) 170

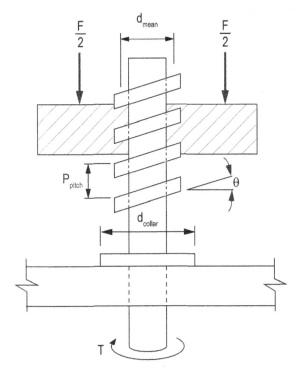

d_{collar} = 1.75 in.
f_{collar} = 0.05
P_{pitch} = 1.75 in.
d_{mean} = 1.50 in.
f_{screw} = 0.08
θ = 3.033°

538. A 2-in.-diameter solid shaft is fixed at Point A and is subject to loading as shown in the figure. Assume the steel is AISI 1035, forged and heat-treated with a yield strength of 81,000 psi, and that the distortion energy theory applies. The load (lb) causing failure (yielding) is most nearly:

(A) 3,860
(B) 4,080
(C) 4,285
(D) 4,550

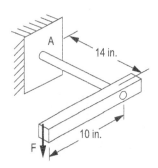

539. A Rockwell testing device uses a ball penetrator to test the surface hardness of a material. Two similar parts are made from the same steel alloy. One is made by machining a solid bar, and the other is sintered powder metal. The diameter of the indentation made in the powder metal part by the tester is larger than the indentation in the machined steel. The hardness reading for the powder metal part will be:

(A) lower than for the machined part

(B) the same as for the machined part

(C) higher than for the machined part

(D) The Rockwell hardness of sintered metals cannot be measured.

540. Aluminum alloy 2024 is to be used on a project. A minimum 0.2% offset yield strength of 55 ksi is required. Per ASTM B 209-4 on the opposite page, the heat treat and final temper required is most nearly:

(A) T42

(B) T62

(C) T351

(D) T851

540. (Continued)

Temper	Specified Thickness, in.	Tensile Strength, ksi		Yield Strength (0.2% offset), ksi		Elongation in 2 in. or 4 × Diameter, min, %	Bend Diameter Factor, N
		min	max	min	max		
				ASTM B209-04, Table 3 Continued			
				Alloy 2024			
O	0.010–0.032	...	32.0	...	14.0	12	0
	0.033–0.063	...	32.0	...	14.0	12	1
	0.064–0.128	...	32.0	...	14.0	12	4
	0.129–0.499	...	32.0	...	14.0	12	6
T3	0.008–0.009	63.0	...	42.0	...	10	4
	0.010–0.020	63.0	...	42.0	...	12	4
	0.021–0.051	63.0	...	42.0	...	15	5
	0.052–0.128	63.0	...	42.0	...	15	6
	0.129–0.249	64.0	...	42.0	...	15	8
T351[E]	0.250–0.499	64.0	...	42.0	...	12	...
	0.500–1.000	63.0	...	42.0	...	8	...
	1.001–1.500	62.0	...	42.0	...	7	...
	1.501–2.000	62.0	...	42.0	...	6	...
	2.001–3.000	60.0	...	42.0	...	4	...
	3.001–4.000	57.0	...	41.0	...	4	...
T361[H]	0.020–0.051	67.0	...	50.0	...	8	4
	0.052–0.062	67.0	...	50.0	...	8	8
	0.063–0.249	68.0	...	51.0	...	9	8
	0.250–0.499	66.0	...	49.0	...	9	...
	0.500	66.0	...	49.0	...	10	...
T4[C]	0.010–0.020	62.0	...	40.0	...	12	4
	0.021–0.051	62.0	...	40.0	...	15	5
	0.052–0.128	62.0	...	40.0	...	15	6
	0.129–0.249	62.0	...	40.0	...	15	8
T42[D]	0.010–0.020	62.0	...	38.0	...	12	4
	0.021–0.051	62.0	...	38.0	...	15	5
	0.052–0.128	62.0	...	38.0	...	15	6
	0.129–0.249	62.0	...	38.0	...	15	8
	0.250–0.499	62.0	...	38.0	...	12	10
	0.500–1.000	61.0	...	38.0	...	8	...
	1.001–1.500	60.0	...	38.0	...	7	...
	1.501–2.000	60.0	...	38.0	...	6	...
	2.001–3.000	58.0	...	38.0	...	4	...
T62[D]	0.010–0.499	64.0	...	50.0	...	5	...
	0.500–2.000	63.0	...	50.0	...	5	...
T72[DI]	0.010–0.249	60.0	...	46.0	...	5	...
T81	0.010–0.249	67.0	...	58.0	...	5	...
T851[E]	0.250–0.499	67.0	...	58.0	...	5	...
	0.500–1.000	66.0	...	58.0	...	5	...
	1.001–1.499	66.0	...	57.0	...	5	...
T861[H]	0.020–0.062	70.0	...	62.0	...	3	...
	0.063–0.249	71.0	...	66.0	...	4	...
	0.250–0.499	70.0	...	64.0	...	4	...
	0.500	70.0	...	64.0	...	4	...
F[F]	0.250–3.000	...	...	...	...	...	...
				Alclad Alloy 2024			
O	0.008–0.009	...	30.0	...	14.0	10	0
	0.010–0.032	...	30.0	...	14.0	12	0
	0.033–0.062	...	30.0	...	14.0	12	1
	0.063–0.249	...	32.0	...	14.0	12	2
	0.250–0.499	...	32.0	...	14.0	12	3
	0.500–1.750	...	32.0[G]	...	...	12	...
T3	0.008–0.009	58.0	...	39.0	...	10	4
	0.010–0.020	59.0	...	39.0	...	12	4

Copyright ASTM International, 100 Barr Harbor Drive, West Conshohocken, PA 19428-2959 USA.

This completes the afternoon session.
Solutions begin on page 89.

AM SOLUTIONS

Answers to the AM Practice Exam

Detailed solutions for each question begin on the next page.

101	C	121	B
102	D	122	C
103	A	123	D
104	A	124	C
105	B	125	D
106	B	126	A
107	D	127	B
108	B	128	B
109	B	129	B
110	C	130	D
111	D	131	D
112	C	132	C
113	D	133	C
114	C	134	A
115	D	135	D
116	B	136	B
117	B	137	C
118	C	138	A
119	A	139	D
120	C	140	B

MACHINE DESIGN AND MATERIALS AM SOLUTIONS

101. Option C shows the position symbol specified, for example in ASME Y14.5, *Dimensioning and Tolerancing.*

THE CORRECT ANSWER IS: (C)

102. To determine the shear load in the thread, the following data must be known: cylinder diameter, piston thickness, piston rod diameter, fluid pressure, and thread size (pitch and length under load).

THE CORRECT ANSWER IS: (D)

103.

Subgroup #	Subgroup Minimum	Subgroup Maximum	Range
1	6.7	8.7	2.0
2	7.0	8.2	1.2
3	6.8	7.9	1.1
4	7.1	8.5	1.4
5	6.9	8.7	1.8
Average range = Rbar = mean of ranges = 1.5			

From **Table 2:**

Need D_4 and D_3 for sample size 4 to get control limits for range

$$D_4 = 2.28$$
$$D_3 = 0$$
$$UCL = D_4 * Rbar = 3.42$$
$$LCL = D_3 * Rbar = 0$$

THE CORRECT ANSWER IS: (A)

104. 80 hr − 10% lost production time = 72 hr
72 hr × 60 units/hr = 4,320 units ⇒ (1 scrap/20 units) × 4,320 units = 216 scrap units
4,320 − 216 units = 4,104 units

THE CORRECT ANSWER IS: (A)

105. If Task C is delayed by 3 days, but has 2 days to spare while waiting on Task D, then the total compensation delay will be 1 day of delivery time.

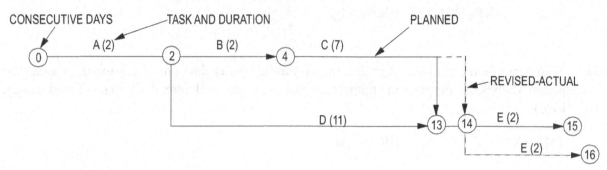

THE CORRECT ANSWER IS: (B)

106. $\dfrac{\text{Good Parts}}{\text{Week}} = \dfrac{12 \text{ units}}{\text{hr}} \left| \dfrac{80 \text{ hr}}{\text{week}} \right| \dfrac{79}{80} = 948$

THE CORRECT ANSWER IS: (B)

107. $1 \text{ ksi} = 6.8948 \text{ MPa}$

$1\sqrt{\text{in.}} = 0.15937\sqrt{\text{m}}$

$1 \text{ ksi}\sqrt{\text{in.}} = 1.0989 \text{ MPa}\sqrt{\text{m}}$

$35 \text{ ksi}\sqrt{\text{in.}} = 38.46 \text{ MPa}\sqrt{\text{m}}$

THE CORRECT ANSWER IS: (D)

MACHINE DESIGN AND MATERIALS AM SOLUTIONS

108. The formula for the critical speed is given as:

$$\text{speed}_{crit} = \frac{215}{L^2}\sqrt{\frac{EIg}{\rho A}}$$

The area moment of inertia is found from $I = \frac{\pi d^4}{64} = \frac{\pi(0.84^4)}{64} = 0.024 \text{ in}^4$.

The cross-sectional area is found from $A = \frac{\pi d^2}{4} = \frac{\pi(0.84^2)}{4} = 0.554 \text{ in}^2$.

The value for E is given as 30,000,000 lb/in^2. The density of steel can be found in many references. Using *Marks' Standard Handbook for Mechanical Engineers*, 8th edition, p. 6-7, an average value for the density of steel is found to be 489 lb/ft^3. This converts to 0.28 lb/in^3.

$$\text{speed}_{crit} = \frac{215}{48^2}\sqrt{\frac{30,000,000 \times 0.024 \times 386.4}{0.28 \times 0.554}}$$

This results in a critical speed of 3,952 rpm.

THE CORRECT ANSWER IS: (B)

109. Structural decomposition is based on the structural organization and makeup of the product.

THE CORRECT ANSWER IS: (B)

MACHINE DESIGN AND MATERIALS AM SOLUTIONS

110. Using an iron-carbon diagram, Option (C) will cool to ferrite and pearlite.

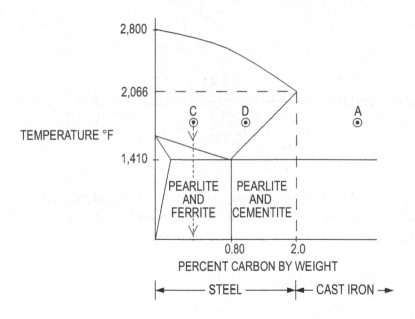

Option (B) is incorrect since AISI 304, a stainless steel, contains numerous alloying components in addition to the iron and carbon shown on this diagram. The last two digits of the AISI material code indicate the weight percent carbon. "95" would be to the right of 0.80 and is outside the pearlite/ferrite region. "40" is to the left of 0.80 and is at the middle of the pearlite/ferrite region, or about 50% of each. Therefore, AISI 1040 meets the requirements of the question.

THE CORRECT ANSWER IS: (C)

MACHINE DESIGN AND MATERIALS AM SOLUTIONS

111. Rod volume = AL = $\pi \dfrac{d^2}{4} L = \pi \dfrac{0.375^2}{4} 10 = 1.105 \text{ in}^3$

Rod weight = rod volume × material density
Strength-to-weight ratio = yield strength/rod weight
Rod cost = rod weight × material cost/lb

Material	Rod Weight	Strength-to-Weight Ratio	Rod Cost
Steel	0.33	144,600	$0.05
Aluminum	0.11	360,000	$0.09
Titanium	0.22	795,000	$0.60
Magnesium	0.07	314,000	$0.06

The two materials meeting the cost requirement are steel and magnesium. Of the two, magnesium has the highest strength-to-weight ratio. Note that the ordering of the strength-to-weight ratio will also be correct if a strength-to-density ratio is used.

THE CORRECT ANSWER IS: (D)

112. $K\delta_s = \dfrac{AE}{\ell}(\alpha \ell \Delta T - \delta_s)$

$\delta_s = \dfrac{\alpha \ell \Delta T}{1 + \dfrac{K\ell}{AE}} = \dfrac{(6 \times 10^{-6})(36)(300)}{1 + \dfrac{(10,000)(36)}{\pi[0.375]30 \times 10^6}} = 0.0628 \text{ in.}$

$F = K\delta_s = (10,000)(0.0628) = 628 \text{ lb}$

THE CORRECT ANSWER IS: (C)

113. Only mild steels exhibit the stress-stain curve shown.

THE CORRECT ANSWER IS: (D)

MACHINE DESIGN AND MATERIALS AM SOLUTIONS

114.

$$\frac{F_c L}{A_c E_c} = \frac{F_s L}{A_s E_s}$$

$$\frac{A_c E_c}{E_s} = \frac{A_s}{F_s} F_c$$

$$\sigma_s = F_s / A_s$$

$$\frac{A_c E_c}{E_s} = \frac{1}{\sigma_s} F_c$$

$$\frac{15.635 \times 3,000,000}{30,000,000} = \frac{1}{\sigma_s} F_c$$

$$F_c = 1.5635 \, \sigma_s$$

$$F = F_c + F_s$$

$$= 1.5635 \, \sigma_s + 4 \, \sigma_s$$

$$= 5.5635 \, \sigma_s = 100,000 \text{ lb}$$

$$\sigma_s = 17,974 \text{ psi}$$

THE CORRECT ANSWER IS: (C)

115. A dielectric union prevents galvanic reaction between different pipe materials.

THE CORRECT ANSWER IS: (D)

MACHINE DESIGN AND MATERIALS AM SOLUTIONS

116. A table or chart conversion between hardness and tensile strength is available in many references. Conversion between Rockwell C and Brinell:

Rockwell C	Brinell (from chart)
28	271
29	279

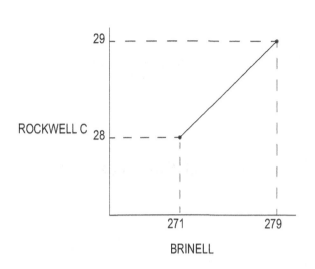

$y = mx + b$

$28 = m(271) + b$

$b = 28 - m(271)$

$29 = m(279) + b$

$29 = m(279) + 28 - m(271)$

$1 = m(8) \Rightarrow m = \frac{1}{8}$

$29 = \frac{1}{8}(279) + b \Rightarrow b = -5.875$

$y = \frac{1}{8}(x) - 5.875$

For 28.8 Rockwell C

$(28.8 + 5.875)\,8 = 277.4$ Brinell

$S_u \approx (500)(BHN)$

$S_u = 138{,}700$ psi

THE CORRECT ANSWER IS: (B)

117.
$$\delta = \alpha L (\Delta t)$$
$$= \left(6 \times 10^{-6} \frac{\text{in.}}{\text{in.-}^\circ\text{F}}\right)(24\,\text{in.})(250^\circ\text{F})$$
$$= 0.036 \text{ in.}$$
$$\sigma = \frac{\delta E}{L}$$
$$= \frac{(0.036 \text{ in.})(30 \times 10^6 \text{ psi})}{24 \text{ in.}}$$
$$= 45{,}000 \text{ psi}$$

THE CORRECT ANSWER IS: (B)

MACHINE DESIGN AND MATERIALS AM SOLUTIONS

118. Angular frequency, $\omega = \sqrt{\dfrac{Kg_c}{m}} = \sqrt{\dfrac{(20\text{ lbf/in.})(12\text{ in./1 ft})[32.2\text{ lbm-ft/(lbf-sec}^2)]}{10\text{ lbm}}} = 27.8\text{ rad/sec}$

Linear frequency, $f = \dfrac{\omega}{2\pi} = \dfrac{27.8\text{ rad/sec}}{2\pi\text{ rad/cycle}} = 4.4\text{ cycles/sec}$

THE CORRECT ANSWER IS: (C)

119. The general expression for damp vibration is

$X_0 = X_1 e^{-\zeta \omega_n t} \sin(\omega_d t + \phi)$

where

ς = damping factor

ω_d = natural damp circular frequency

ω_N = natural circular frequency

X_t = amplitude of vibration

t = time

ϕ = phase angle

$T_d = \dfrac{2\pi}{\omega_d} = \dfrac{2\pi}{2.2} = 2.85\text{ sec}$

THE CORRECT ANSWER IS: (A)

120. Maximum deflection for a rotating unbalance.

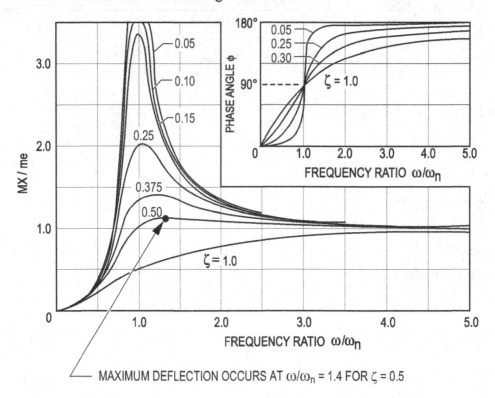

MAXIMUM DEFLECTION OCCURS AT $\omega/\omega_n = 1.4$ FOR $\zeta = 0.5$

THE CORRECT ANSWER IS: (C)

MACHINE DESIGN AND MATERIALS AM SOLUTIONS

121.

$$J_u = \frac{f(3g^2 + f^2)}{6}$$

$$J = 0.707\, h\, J_u = \frac{0.707}{6} h\, f(3g^2 + f^2)$$

$$r = \frac{\sqrt{f^2 + g^2}}{2}$$

$$\tau'' = \frac{mr}{J} = \frac{6\,We\sqrt{f^2 + g^2}}{2(0.707)\,h\,f(3g^2 + f^2)}$$

$$h = \frac{6\,We\sqrt{f^2 + g^2}}{1.414\,\tau''\,f(3g^2 + f^2)}$$

$$= \frac{6(4{,}500\text{ lb})(6\text{ in.})\sqrt{1.5^2 + 6^2}}{1.414\,(12{,}000)(1.5\text{ in.})(3\times 6^2 + 2.25)} = 0.357\text{ in.}$$

$$= 3/8 \text{ in.}$$

W = 4,500 lb
e = 6 in.
g = 6 in.
f = 1.5 in.

THE CORRECT ANSWER IS: (B)

122.

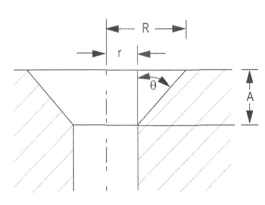

$R = \varnothing/2 = 0.78\text{ in.}/2 = 0.39\text{ in.}$
$r = \text{I.D.}/2 = 5/16\text{ in.}/2 = 0.156\text{ in.}$
$\theta = 82°/2 = 41°$

$L = R - r = 0.39 - 0.156 = 0.234$ in.

$A = \dfrac{L}{\tan\theta} = \dfrac{0.234}{\tan 41°} = 0.269$ in.

Detail of outer part of countersink

THE CORRECT ANSWER IS: (C)

MACHINE DESIGN AND MATERIALS AM SOLUTIONS

123. Draw a free-body diagram.

Forces due to load:

Plus forces due to torsion:

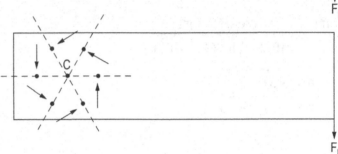

Add vectors:

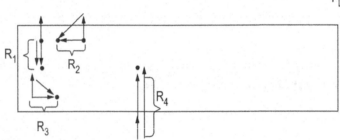

Bolt 4 has additive vectors and the greatest shear stress.

THE CORRECT ANSWER IS: (D)

124. $k_b = \dfrac{AE}{L} = \dfrac{0.142\,(30 \times 10^6)}{1} = 4.26 \times 10^6$

$k_b = k_m$ (given)

Preload = 5,000 lb   Applied load = $p_i A = 500\,\dfrac{\pi(12)^2}{4} = 56{,}500$

Applied load per bolt = 7,070 lb

Bolt force: $F_b = F_i + \dfrac{k_b}{k_b + k_m}(7{,}070) = 5{,}000 + \dfrac{1}{2}(7{,}070) = 8{,}535$ lb

Bolt stress: $\sigma_b = \dfrac{F_b}{A_s} = \dfrac{8{,}535}{0.142} = 60{,}100$ psi

THE CORRECT ANSWER IS: (C)

MACHINE DESIGN AND MATERIALS AM SOLUTIONS

125. Direct shear force $F_1 = 500/3 = 167$ lb

Centroid of bolt group will be at bolt B

$r_A = r_c = 6$ in.

$M = 500(19) = 9{,}500$ in.-lb

Secondary shear force $\quad F_B = 0$

$$F_A = \frac{-9{,}500(6)}{(2)(36)} = -792 \text{ lb}$$

$$F_C = \frac{9{,}500(6)}{(2)(36)} = 792 \text{ lb}$$

$F_{max} = 792 + 167 = 959$ lb

THE CORRECT ANSWER IS: (D)

126. Two times

Look up the tensile strength of each bolt grade in a reference. According to *Marks' Standard Handbook for Mechanical Engineers*, the following tensile strengths were found.

SAE Grade 2, 74 kpsi

SAE Grade 8, 150 kpsi

Ratio = $\dfrac{150 \text{ kpsi}}{74 \text{ kpsi}} = 2$

THE CORRECT ANSWER IS: (A)

127.

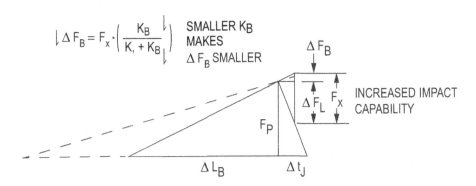

Increasing the length of the bolt does not affect joint preload or joint compression.

THE CORRECT ANSWER IS: (B)

128.

$$\tau = \frac{VQ}{It}$$

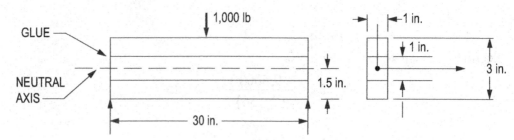

$I = \dfrac{bH^3}{12} = \dfrac{(1)(3)^3}{12} = 2.25 \text{ in}^4$

$t = 1$ in. wide
$V = 1,000$ lb vertical shear
Q (first moment of inertia) at location of shear stress
$= 1 \times 1 \times 1 = 1$

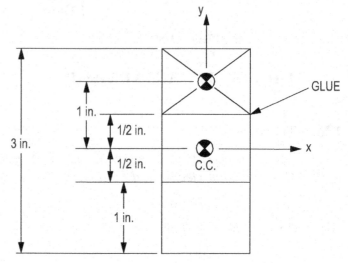

$$\tau = \frac{VQ}{It}$$

$$= \frac{(1{,}000 \text{ lb})(1 \text{ in}^3)}{(2.25 \text{ in}^4)(1 \text{ in.})} = 444 \text{ lb/in}^2$$

THE CORRECT ANSWER IS: (B)

MACHINE DESIGN AND MATERIALS AM SOLUTIONS

129.  Bevel weld

Field weld

THE CORRECT ANSWER IS: (B)

130. Shear stress $\tau = \dfrac{F}{bt_e}$

t_e = effective throat size = 0.707y
b = length of weld
b = π(3)
Factor of safety of 4

$\left(\dfrac{24,000}{4}\right)(\pi)(3)(0.707)(y) = 19.600$ lb

$y = \dfrac{19,600 \text{ lb}}{\left(\dfrac{24,000}{4}\right)(\pi)(3)(0.707)} = 0.49$

THE CORRECT ANSWER IS: (D)

MACHINE DESIGN AND MATERIALS AM SOLUTIONS

131. Grade 5 rod has a yield of 81,000 lb/in^2

For a 1 1/4-7 thread the tensile stress area is 0.696 in^2. A factor of safety of 4 is required.

$$\left(\frac{P}{0.969}\right) = \left(\frac{81,000 \text{ lb/in}^2}{4}\right) \Rightarrow P = \left(0.969 \text{ in}^2\right)\left(\frac{81,000 \text{ lb/in}^2}{4}\right)$$

$$P = 19,622 \text{ lb}$$

THE CORRECT ANSWER IS: (D)

132. The shear strength of the epoxy is 1,500 psi. The coverage area of the epoxy A = (80%)(L)(W)(2), where the overlap length is 2 in., the overlap width is 2 in., and both sides of the center plate are glued.

$$S = \frac{P}{A} \Rightarrow 1,500 \text{ psi} = \frac{P}{0.8(2)(2)(2)} = \frac{P}{6.4}$$

$$P = 9,600 \text{ lb}$$

THE CORRECT ANSWER IS: (C)

133.

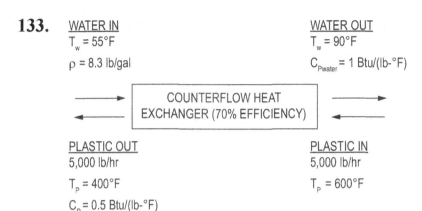

WATER IN
$T_w = 55°F$
$\rho = 8.3$ lb/gal

WATER OUT
$T_w = 90°F$
$C_{P_{water}} = 1$ Btu/(lb-°F)

PLASTIC OUT
5,000 lb/hr
$T_p = 400°F$
$C_p = 0.5$ Btu/(lb-°F)

PLASTIC IN
5,000 lb/hr
$T_p = 600°F$

Heat given up by plastic = heat gained by water

For plastic:
$$\begin{aligned} Q &= \dot{m}C_p\Delta T \\ &= (5{,}000 \text{ lb/hr})[0.5 \text{ Btu/(lb-°F)}](200°F) \\ &= 500{,}000 \text{ Btu/hr} \end{aligned}$$

For water:
$$Q = \dot{m}C_p\Delta T$$
$$\dot{m} = \frac{500{,}000 \text{ Btu/hr}}{[1 \text{ Btu/(lb-°F)}](35°F)}$$
$$= 14{,}285.7 \text{ lb/hr}$$

Conversion from lb/hr to gpm:
$$(14{,}285.7 \text{ lb/hr})\left(\frac{1 \text{ gal}}{8.3 \text{ lb}}\right)\left(\frac{1 \text{ hr}}{60 \text{ min}}\right) = 28.68 \text{ gpm (no efficiency)}$$

Account for efficiency:
$28.68 \text{ gpm}/0.70 = 40.72 \text{ gpm}$

THE CORRECT ANSWER IS: (C)

MACHINE DESIGN AND MATERIALS AM SOLUTIONS

134. 1. Determine minimum centerline of holes: $\mathcal{C}_L = 2.4 - 1.2 - 2(0.05) = 1.1$
       2. Determine the maximum outside diameter of holes: $D_{max} = 0.9$
       3. Determine minimum distance between surfaces: $1.1 - 0.9 = 0.2$

THE CORRECT ANSWER IS: (A)

135. Let diametrical pitch, P = 6

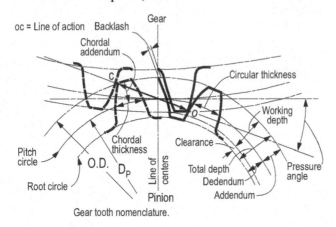
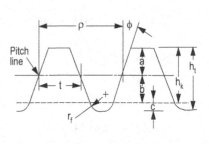

Avallone, Eugene A., and Theodore Baumeister III, eds., *Mark's Standard Handbook for Mechanical Engineers*, 9 ed., McGraw-Hill, 1986, p. 8-91.

$$d_1 = \frac{N_1}{P} = \frac{42}{6} = 7.0 \text{ in. (diameter of spur gear 1)}$$

$$n_2 = n_1 \frac{N_1}{N_2} \rightarrow N_2 = N_1 \frac{n_1}{n_2} = 42 \frac{1{,}800}{1{,}080} = 70 \text{ teeth (number of teeth on gear 1)}$$

$$d_2 = \frac{N_2}{P} = \frac{70}{6} = 11.67 \text{ in. (diameter of spur gear 2)}$$

$$a = \frac{1}{P} = \frac{1}{6} = 0.167 \text{ in. (height of addendum)}$$

Case diameter (remembering to add the addendum on both sides)

$$\text{case} = d_1 + d_2 + 2a + \text{clearance}$$
$$= 7 + 11.67 + 2 \times 0.167 + 0.50 = 19.5 \text{ in.}$$

THE CORRECT ANSWER IS: (D)

MACHINE DESIGN AND MATERIALS AM SOLUTIONS

136. A 5/8 ANSI bolt is 1.083 in. across the corners, so D must be larger than that by a reasonable amount to accommodate the angle.
Hole diameter d must be 0.050 over nominal diameter per Table 3, or 5/8 + 0.050 = 0.675 in.
Radius r must be 0.060 per Table 3.
Wedge thickness T equals half-nominal bolt diameter, or 0.313.

THE CORRECT ANSWER IS: (B)

137.

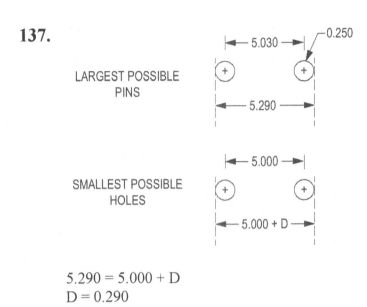

$5.290 = 5.000 + D$
$D = 0.290$

THE CORRECT ANSWER IS: (C)

138. ASTM sets testing standards for materials including calibration, minimum tolerances, and applicable formulas.

THE CORRECT ANSWER IS: (A)

MACHINE DESIGN AND MATERIALS AM SOLUTIONS

139. When an object is twisted, shearing stress occurs. At the same time, at 45° from the longitudinal axis, tensile and compressive stresses occur resulting from the shearing stress. The strain gages measure tensile or compressive strain resulting from tensile or compressive stress simultaneously generated with the shearing stress. The strain is at a maximum at 45° and therefore the gages are best oriented at that angle.

THE CORRECT ANSWER IS: (D)

140. Enter the table at the row for nominal diameters from 1.19–1.58. The lower bound on shaft diameter is +0.0018 in.
∴ d = 1.50 + 0.0018 = 1.5018 in.

THE CORRECT ANSWER IS: (B)

PM SOLUTIONS

Answers to the Machine Design and Materials PM Practice Exam

Detailed solutions for each question begin on the next page.

501	D	521	A
502	D	522	B
503	C	523	B
504	A	524	A
505	C	525	B
506	B	526	C
507	C	527	C
508	D	528	A
509	C	529	D
510	B	530	C
511	A	531	D
512	D	532	C
513	A	533	D
514	A	534	D
515	A	535	D
516	B	536	B
517	B	537	A
518	A	538	A
519	D	539	A
520	D	540	D

MACHINE DESIGN AND MATERIALS PM SOLUTIONS

501. The belt friction formula:

$$P/W = e^{f\theta}$$

where: f = the coefficient of friction, and
θ = the angle of wrap

Therefore: $P = We^{0.35 \times 3.14159}$
$= (50 \text{ lbf})(e^{0.35 \times 3.14159})$
$= 150 \text{ lbf}$

THE CORRECT ANSWER IS: (D)

502. (1) $\vec{v}_C = \vec{v}_A + \vec{v}_{C/A} = \vec{v}_A + \vec{w}_{AB} \times \vec{r}_{C/A} = \vec{v}_A + \vec{w}_{AB} \times \frac{1}{2}\vec{r}_{B/A}$

(2) $\vec{v}_B = \vec{v}_A + \vec{v}_{B/A} = \vec{v}_A + \vec{w}_{AB} \times \vec{r}_{B/A}$

From (2):

$$4\hat{j} = -3\hat{i} + \vec{w}_{AB} \times \vec{r}_{B/A} \Rightarrow \vec{w}_{AB} \times \vec{r}_{B/A} = 3\hat{i} + 4\hat{j}$$

Substituting in (1) $\vec{v}_C = -3\hat{i} + \frac{1}{2}(3\hat{i} + 4\hat{j})$

$$= \left(\frac{-3\hat{i} + 4\hat{j}}{2}\right) \text{m/s}$$

$$|v_C| = \frac{5}{2} = 2.5 \text{ m/s}^2$$

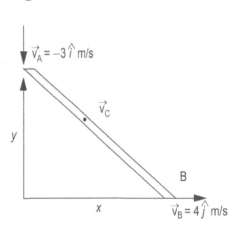

THE CORRECT ANSWER IS: (D)

503. Single-row ball bearing: assume the shaft to be simply supported.

Weight of disk, W	41 lb
Elastic modulus, E	28,600,000 psi
Acceleration due to gravity, g	386.4 in./sec²
Span length of shaft, L	18 in.
Shaft diameter, d	1.18 in.
Bending moment of inertia of I	$I = \dfrac{\pi d^4}{64} = \dfrac{\pi(1.181)^4}{64} 0.09549 \text{ in}^4$
Shaft stiffness in lateral direction	$k = 48 \times E \times I/L^3 = 22,478 \text{ lb/in.}$
Natural frequency	$60/(2\pi) \times \sqrt{(kg/W)} = 4,395 \text{ rpm}$

THE CORRECT ANSWER IS: (C)

MACHINE DESIGN AND MATERIALS PM SOLUTIONS

504. Dimension a is needed to determine the moment reactions. Dimension b is needed to determine torque reactions. Dimension c is not needed.

THE CORRECT ANSWER IS: (A)

505. With 400 lbf acting on the rear wheel and with constant velocity, an equal resistance force must be acting against the front of the car, effective at the center of gravity. At the front wheel there is only the normal force from the road. All moments at the front wheel must sum to zero. Looking at one side of the car (supporting half its weight):

ΣM_{front} = (100 in.) N_{rear} – (18 in.)(400 lbf) – (50 in.)(1,200 lbf) = 0
N_{rear} = 672 lbf

THE CORRECT ANSWER IS: (C)

506. $\tan \theta = \dfrac{5}{12}$

$= 0.4166$

$\theta = 24.6°$

$\sum F_n = 0$

$N = W \cos \theta$

$\sum F_t = 0$

$\mu_s N = W \sin \theta$

$\mu_s W \cos \theta = W \sin \theta$

$\mu_s = \dfrac{\sin \theta}{\cos \theta} = \tan \theta = \tan 24.6°$

$\mu_s = 0.46$

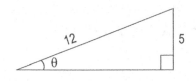

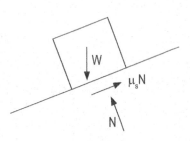

THE CORRECT ANSWER IS: (B)

MACHINE DESIGN AND MATERIALS PM SOLUTIONS

507.

$$a = \frac{v_o^2}{2s} = \frac{\left(65 \times \frac{5,280}{3,600}\right)^2}{2 \times 400}$$

$$= 11.36 \text{ ft/sec}^2$$

$$\alpha = \frac{a}{r} = \frac{11.36}{\left(\frac{28}{12 \times 2}\right)} = 9.74 \text{ rad/s}^2$$

THE CORRECT ANSWER IS: (C)

508. $v_y^2 = (v_y)_0^2 + 2a_c(y - y_0)$

where $v_y = 0$
$a_c = -32.2 \text{ ft/sec}^2$
$y = 75 \text{ ft}$
$y_0 = -25 \text{ ft}$

$0 = (v_y)_0^2 + 2(-32.2 \text{ ft/sec}^2)(75 \text{ ft} - (-25 \text{ ft}))$

$(v_y)_0^2 = 6,440 \text{ ft}^2/\text{sec}^2$

$(v_y)_0 = 80.25 \text{ ft/sec}$

$v_0 = \frac{80.25 \text{ ft/sec}}{\sin 40°}$

$v_0 = 125 \text{ ft/sec}$

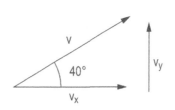

THE CORRECT ANSWER IS: (D)

MACHINE DESIGN AND MATERIALS PM SOLUTIONS

509. Using conservation of momentum, solve for the initial velocity of the bullet-block system.

$m_{bullet} v_{bullet} = (m_{bullet} + m_{block}) v_{system}$

$(0.00324)(610) = (0.570) v_{system}$

$v_{system} = 3.47$ m/s

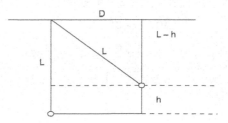

Use conservation of energy to solve for the height the system moves.

$KE_i = PE_f$

$1/2(m_{bullet} + m_{block}) v_{system}^2 = (m_{bullet} + m_{block}) gh$

$h = (1/2)(3.47)^2 / 9.81$

$\quad = 0.612$ m

Using geometry and Pythagorean theorem, solve for the horizontal distance D.

$D^2 + (L-h)^2 = L^2$

$D = \sqrt{L^2 - (L-h)^2} = \sqrt{2^2 - (2-0.612)^2} = 1.44$ m

THE CORRECT ANSWER IS: (C)

510. Force on ceiling = mg.

Tension on chains: $mg = 2T \sin 60°$

$T = \dfrac{mg}{2 \sin 60°}$

Horizontal force on each tong handle, $F_{Ht} = T \cos 60° = \dfrac{mg}{2 \tan 60°}$

Horizontal force at each tong clamp, $N = \dfrac{D_1}{D_2} F_{Ht} = \left(\dfrac{D_1}{D_2}\right)\left(\dfrac{mg}{2 \tan 60°}\right)$

Friction force holding block up:

$2\mu N = mg$

$\mu_{min} = \dfrac{mg}{2N} = \dfrac{D_2}{D_1} \tan 60° = \dfrac{7}{30} \tan 60° = 0.4$

THE CORRECT ANSWER IS: (B)

MACHINE DESIGN AND MATERIALS PM SOLUTIONS

511. $\Sigma M_A = 0$

$R_B(6) = P(10)$

$R_B = 1.667\,P$

$\Sigma F_y = 0$

$R_A = 0.667\,P$

$M_{max} = (6\text{ ft})(0.667)P$

$M_{max} = (4\text{ ft})(P)$

$\sigma = \dfrac{Mc}{I}$

$M = \dfrac{\sigma I}{c} = \dfrac{(36{,}000\text{ psi})(35.5\text{ in}^4)}{3\text{ in.}}$

$\quad = 426{,}000\text{ in.-lbf}$

$(4\text{ ft})(P) = 426{,}000\text{ in.-lbf}$

$P = \dfrac{426{,}000\text{ in.-lbf}}{(4\text{ ft})(12\text{ in./ft})}$

$\quad = 8{,}875\text{ lbf}$

Include factor of safety

$P = 8{,}875/2.5$

$\quad = 3{,}550\text{ lbf}$

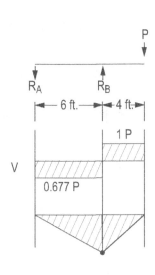

THE CORRECT ANSWER IS: (A)

512. The elongation of the rod is a linear function of stress from 0 to 70,000 psi and is 0.012 in./in. when the stress is 70,000 psi.

Stress = force/area = (2,300 lbf)/[(3.14159)(0.25 in. × 0.25 in.)]
   = 11,700 psi for the rod as loaded.

Unit elongation = (11,700 psi/70,000 psi)(0.012 in./in. at S = 70,000 psi)
   = 0.002 in./in.

For the 6-in.-long rod, the elongation is (6 in.)(0.002 in./in.) = 0.012 in.

THE CORRECT ANSWER IS: (D)

MACHINE DESIGN AND MATERIALS PM SOLUTIONS

513.

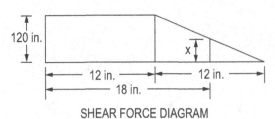

SHEAR FORCE DIAGRAM

$$\frac{x}{6} = \frac{120}{12} \qquad \therefore x = 60 \text{ lb}$$

THE CORRECT ANSWER IS: (A)

514.

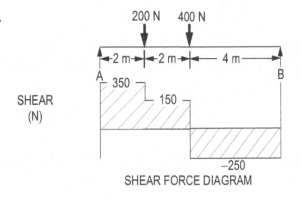

SHEAR FORCE DIAGRAM

$\Sigma M_B = 0$

$-8A + 1,200 + 1,600 = 0$

$8A = 2,800$

$A = 350 \text{ N}$

$B = 600 - 350 = 250 \text{ N}$

Maximum moment = 1,000 N·m

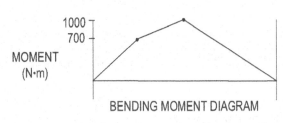

BENDING MOMENT DIAGRAM

THE CORRECT ANSWER IS: (A)

515. Of the given alternatives, only a change in the modulus of elasticity will decrease the deflection.

THE CORRECT ANSWER IS: (A)

MACHINE DESIGN AND MATERIALS PM SOLUTIONS

516. Check compression

$\sigma = P/A$

Allowable force, $P_{all} = \sigma_{all} A = (432 \times 10^6 \text{ N/m}^2)^{(0.100 \text{ in.})(0.25 \text{ m})}$
$P_{all} = 10,800,000$ N

$\sigma_e = \dfrac{\pi^2 E}{(L/k)^2}$

$P_{cr} = \dfrac{\pi^2 E \tau}{l_{eff}^2}$

$I = \dfrac{bh^3}{12} = \dfrac{(0.250)(0.100)^3}{12}$

$P_{cr} = \dfrac{\pi^2 (70 \times 10^9)(2.083 \times 10^{-5})}{(2)^2}$

$I = 2.083 \times 10^{-5} \text{ m}^{-4}$

$P_{cr} = 3,594,670$ N

$l_{eff} = 1$ m

$P_{cr} = \dfrac{\pi^2 (70 \times 10^9)(2.083 \times 10^{-5})}{1^2}$

$P_{cr} = 14,376,282$ N

Failure is increased by $\dfrac{10,800,000}{3,599,070} = 3.0$

THE CORRECT ANSWER IS: (B)

517. Torsional stiffness $= \dfrac{T}{\theta} = \dfrac{GJ}{L}$

$= \dfrac{90 \times 10^3 \times (\pi/32) \times 50^4}{300}$

$= 184 \times 10^6$ N•mm/rad

$= 184 \times 10^3$ N•m/rad

THE CORRECT ANSWER IS: (B)

MACHINE DESIGN AND MATERIALS PM SOLUTIONS

518. For steel, fatigue stress S_f is related to cycles of life N by $S_f = a \times N^b$

$S_{f1} = 90,000$ psi, $N_1 = 1,000$ cycles; $S_{f2} = 50,000$ psi, $N_2 = 1,000,000$ cycles

Substituting these values and solving:

$$b = \log(S_{f1}/S_{f2})/\log(N_1/N_2) = -0.085$$
$$a = S_{f1}/N_1^b = 162,000 \text{ psi}$$

therefore, when:

$$S_{f3} = 70,000 \text{ psi}$$
$$N_3 = (S_{f3}/a)^{(1/b)} = 19,173 \text{ cycles}$$

THE CORRECT ANSWER IS: (A)

519. Point (5) is outside the area of acceptable design (fatigue failure).

THE CORRECT ANSWER IS: (D)

520. The von Mises failure criterion predicts failure when $\sigma' = S_{yt}$, where $\sigma' = \sqrt{\sigma_1^2 + \sigma_2^2 - \sigma_1\sigma_2}$ for biaxial loading, which is the case with this thin-walled cylinder, σ_1 is the hoop stress, and σ_2 is the longitudinal stress.

$$\sigma_1 = \frac{pr}{t} = \frac{3 \text{ MPa} \times \frac{1,000,000 \text{ Pa}}{1 \text{ MPa}} \times \frac{1 \text{ m}}{2}}{1 \text{cm}\left(\frac{1 \text{ m}}{100 \text{ cm}}\right)} = 150 \text{ MPa}$$

$$\sigma_2 = \frac{pr}{2t} = \frac{\sigma_h}{2} = 75 \text{ MPa}$$

$$\sigma' = \sqrt{(150 \text{ MPa})^2 + (75 \text{ MPa})^2 - (150 \text{ MPa})(75 \text{ MPa})} = 130 \text{ MPa}$$

$$FS = \frac{S_{yt}}{\sigma'} = \frac{450 \text{ MPa}}{130 \text{ MPa}} = 3.46$$

THE CORRECT ANSWER IS: (D)

MACHINE DESIGN AND MATERIALS PM SOLUTIONS

521. $t = r_i \left(\sqrt{\dfrac{\sigma_\theta + P}{\sigma_\theta - P}} - 1 \right)$

$= 12 \left(\sqrt{\dfrac{20,000 + 7,500}{20,000 - 7,500}} - 1 \right)$

$= 5.80$

THE CORRECT ANSWER IS: (A)

522. $\dfrac{L_1}{L_2} = \left(\dfrac{F_2}{F_1} \right)^3$

$\dfrac{F_2}{F_1} = \left(\dfrac{L_1}{L_2} \right)^{1/3}$

$L_1 = (180,000 \text{ min})(500 \text{ rev/min}) = 90 \times 10^6 \text{ revolutions}$

$L_2 = (268,000 \text{ min})(10 \text{ rad/sec} \times \text{rev}/2\pi \times 60 \text{ sec/min}) = 25.61 \times 10^6 \text{ revolutions}$

$F_1 = 75 \text{ lb}$

$F_2 = (75) \left(\dfrac{90 \times 10^6}{25.61 \times 10^6} \right)^{1/3} = 114.1 \text{ lb}$

THE CORRECT ANSWER IS: (B)

523. With all other factors the same, reducing the number of ring gear teeth will:
- increase rear wheel rpm $\Rightarrow$ increased vehicle speed
- reduce rear wheel torque $\Rightarrow$ reduced vehicle acceleration

THE CORRECT ANSWER IS: (B)

524.

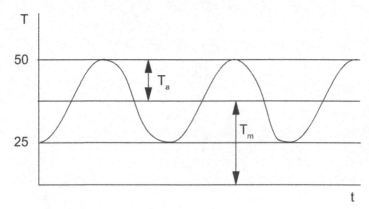

$T_m = \dfrac{50+25}{2} = 37.5$ lb-in.

$T_a = \dfrac{50-25}{2} = 12.5$ lb-in.

THE CORRECT ANSWER IS: (A)

MACHINE DESIGN AND MATERIALS PM SOLUTIONS

525. Pinion torque = $\dfrac{(\text{hp})63,025}{n} = \dfrac{10(63,025)}{1,200} = 525.2$ in.-lb

Pinion radius = $\dfrac{N_1}{2P_d} = \dfrac{20}{12} = 1.66$ in.

Force = $\dfrac{\text{torque}}{\text{radius}} = \dfrac{525.2}{1.66} = 316.41$ lb

where pitch angle = $\tan^{-1}\dfrac{a}{N}$

$= \tan^{-1}\dfrac{20}{40}$

$= 26.56°$

∴ Thrust load = $316.4 \times \tan 20 \times \sin 26.56 = 51.27$ lb

THE CORRECT ANSWER IS: (B)

526. $K = \dfrac{d^4 G}{8 D^3 N}$

where: d = wire diameter
D = spring diameter
N = number of active coils
G = shear modulus
K = spring constant

$N_{st} = N_{br}; \quad D_{st}^3 = D_{br}^3; \quad K_{st} = K_{br}$

$\therefore \dfrac{d_{st}^4 G_{st}}{8 D_{st}^3 N_{st}} = \dfrac{d_{br}^4 G_{br}}{8 D_{br}^3 N_{br}} \Rightarrow d_{st}^4 G_{st} = d_{br}^4 G_{br} \Rightarrow d_{br} = d_{st} \sqrt[4]{G_{st}/G_{br}}$

$d_{br} = 0.15 \sqrt[4]{\dfrac{11 \times 10^6}{5.5 \times 10^6}} = 0.18$ in.

THE CORRECT ANSWER IS: (C)

MACHINE DESIGN AND MATERIALS PM SOLUTIONS

527. Solid height = 10(0.1055) = 1.055 in.

Free height = 3
Max δ = 3 − 1.055 = 1.945 in.
$K = \dfrac{P}{\delta} = 20$
$P = K\delta = 20(1.945) = 39$ lb

THE CORRECT ANSWER IS: (C)

528. Angle of contact = 135° = 2.36 radians

$T_1 = 80 \times 4 = 320$ lb

$\dfrac{320}{T_2} = e^{0.25 \times 2.36} \quad \Rightarrow T_2 = 178$ lb

Resultant force = 320 − 178 = 142 lb

Belt velocity = $\dfrac{250 \times 2\pi}{60} \times \dfrac{21}{12} = 45.8$ fps

Work done = force × velocity = 142 × 45.8 = 6,505 ft-lbf/sec

$hp = \dfrac{6,505}{550} = 11.8$ hp

THE CORRECT ANSWER IS: (A)

529. T = 320 N·m, diameter = 40 mm

Shear force at key = $\dfrac{T}{r} = \dfrac{320 \times 10^3}{20} = 16 \times 10^3$ N

Allowable shear stress = $\tau_{ys} = \dfrac{S_y}{2} = \dfrac{200}{2} = 100$ MPa

Shear stress at key = $\dfrac{\text{shear force}}{L \times W} = \dfrac{16 \times 10^3}{L \times 8} = 100 \dfrac{N}{mm^2}$

L = 20 mm

THE CORRECT ANSWER IS: (D)

MACHINE DESIGN AND MATERIALS PM SOLUTIONS

530. The basic equation is $E = \dfrac{\sigma}{\varepsilon}$, from which $E = \dfrac{PL}{A\delta}$.

The stiffness k is defined as $k = \dfrac{P}{\delta}$.

$\therefore k = \dfrac{EA}{L}$

It is reasonable to use an average cross-sectional diameter for deformation.

$D_{average} = \dfrac{1 + 0.84}{2} = 0.92$

$\therefore k = \dfrac{30,000,000 \times \pi \times 0.92^2}{48 \times 4}$

$= 415,476$ lb/in.

THE CORRECT ANSWER IS: (C)

531. Buckling factor of safety = 1.5
$P_{cr} = \pi^2 E I/l^2$
$I = \dfrac{\pi d^4}{64}$
Assume pinned ends.

$(500)(1.5) = \pi^2 \dfrac{(30 \times 10^6)}{7.07^2}\left(\dfrac{\pi d^4}{64}\right)$

$750 = 290,774 \, d^4$

$d = 0.225$ in.

Check compressive stress required diameter.
Yield factor of safety = 2.0
$P = \sigma A$
$(500)(2) = (60,000 \, \pi \, d^2)/4$
$1,000 = 47,124 \, d^2$
$d = 0.146$ in.
Thus, buckling is the critical design load.

THE CORRECT ANSWER IS: (D)

MACHINE DESIGN AND MATERIALS PM SOLUTIONS

532. According to *Marks' Standard Handbook for Mechanical Engineers*, 9th edition, p. 15-7, the combined resistance of a number of series-connected resistors is the sum of their separate resistances.

$$R_e = R_1 + R_2 + R_3$$

THE CORRECT ANSWER IS: (C)

533. The rod has pinned ends → C = 1

$$\sigma_e = \frac{\pi^2 E}{\left(\frac{CL}{K}\right)^2}$$

Factor of safety of 2

$$\frac{\sigma_y}{FS} = \frac{73{,}000}{2} = 36{,}500 \text{ lb/in}^2$$

$$\frac{CL}{K} = \sqrt{\frac{\pi^2 E}{\sigma_e}}$$

$$K = \frac{CL}{\sqrt{\frac{\pi^2 E}{\sigma_e}}} = \frac{(1)(50 \text{ in.})}{\sqrt{\frac{\pi^2 (30 \times 10^6 \text{ lb/in}^2)}{36{,}500 \text{ lb/in}^2}}}$$

$$K = 0.555$$

$$K = \sqrt{\frac{I}{A}} = \sqrt{\frac{\frac{\pi}{4}r^4}{\pi r^2}} = \sqrt{\frac{r^2}{4}}$$

$$r = \sqrt{(K^2)(4)}$$

$r = 1.11$ in.
Diameter = 2r = 2.22

Check slenderness:

$$\frac{L}{K} = \frac{50}{0.555} = 90 \text{ Slenderness ratio 80 to 120}$$

Check compressive yield strength:

$$\frac{\left(\frac{\pi}{4}\right)(2.75)^2 (3{,}000)}{\left(\frac{\pi}{4}\right)(2.22)^2} = 4{,}603 \text{ (less than half yield so OK)}$$

THE CORRECT ANSWER IS: (D)

MACHINE DESIGN AND MATERIALS PM SOLUTIONS

534. $I = \dfrac{(sf)(P)}{(V)\eta(pf)}$

$I = \dfrac{(1.0)(7,457)}{(230)(0.65)(0.80)} = 62.3\ A$

Service factor, sf = 1.0 at full load
Power, P = 10 hp × 0.7457 kW/hp × 1,000 W/kW
= 7,457 W
Voltage, V = 230 V
Efficiency, η = 0.65
Power factor, pf = 0.80

THE CORRECT ANSWER IS: (D)

535. Using the pump similarity laws, power is directly proportional to the cube of the speed.

$P_2 = P_1(S_2/S_1)^3$

$P_2 = 1{,}000\ hp\ (1{,}000\ rpm/1{,}750\ rpm)^3$

$= 186\ hp$

$= 139\ kW$

THE CORRECT ANSWER IS: (D)

536. First solve for the equivalent coefficient of friction using the equation provided. Make sure to convert the contact angle from degrees to radians.

$\phi = 80° = 1.4\ rad$

$\mu' = \dfrac{\mu\left(\sin\dfrac{\phi}{2}\right)}{\phi + \sin\phi} = 0.864$

The braking force is given by $F_B = \mu'P = 130N$

The braking torque is given by $T_B = F_B \cdot D/2 = 26Nm$

The angular acceleration due to braking: $\Sigma T = I\alpha = (mr^2/2)\ \alpha = -26$

$\alpha = -130\ rad/s^2$

Solve for the time: $W_f = W_0 + \alpha t$
$W_f = 0$
$W_0 = 50\ rad/s$
$0 = 50 - 130t$
$t = 0.3785\ sec$

THE CORRECT ANSWER IS: (B)

MACHINE DESIGN AND MATERIALS PM SOLUTIONS

537. The torque required to turn against a load for the collar is given by

$$T_c = \frac{Ff_c d_c}{2}$$

$$= \frac{(1,700 \text{ lb})(0.05)(1.75 \text{ in.})}{2}$$

$$= 74.3 \text{ lb-in.}$$

The torque required to turn a square thread against a load is given by

$$T_R = \frac{Fd_m}{2}\left(\frac{\ell + \pi f_s d_m}{\pi d_m - f_s \ell}\right)$$

where

Lead, $\ell = \pi d_m \tan\theta$

$= \pi(1.50)(\tan 3.033)$

$= 0.249$ for one thread. Problem states triple thread.

$\ell = (3)(0.249) = 0.75$

$$= \frac{(1,700 \text{ lb})(1.5 \text{ in.})}{2} \times \left(\frac{0.75 + \pi(0.08)(1.5)}{\pi(1.5) - (0.08)(0.75)}\right)$$

$$= 1,275\left(\frac{1.126}{4.65}\right)$$

$$= 308.7 \text{ lb-in.}$$

Total torque to turn the screw is given by

$T = T_c + T_R$

$= 74.3 + 308.7$

$= 383$ lb-in.

THE CORRECT ANSWER IS: (A)

538. $M = (14 \text{ in.})(F)$

$T = (10 \text{ in.})(F)$

$$\sigma' = \frac{Mc}{I} = \frac{32M}{\pi d^3} = \frac{32(14\text{ F})}{\pi(2 \text{ in.})^3} = 17.825 \text{ F}$$

$$\tau_{xy} = \frac{Tr}{J} = \frac{16T}{\pi d^3} = \frac{16(10\text{ F})}{\pi(2 \text{ in.})^3} = 6.366 \text{ F}$$

$$\sigma' = \sqrt{(\sigma_x^2 + 3\tau_{xy}^2)} = \sqrt{(17.8 \text{ F})^2 + 3(6.366 \text{ F})^2} = F\sqrt{317.7 + 121.6} = 20.96 \text{ F}$$

$$\sigma' = S_y = 20.96 \text{ F} \Rightarrow F\frac{S_y}{20.96} = \frac{81,000}{20.96} = 3,864.5 \text{ lb}$$

THE CORRECT ANSWER IS: (A)

MACHINE DESIGN AND MATERIALS PM SOLUTIONS

539. Porosity causes the ball to indent further and give a larger indentation diameter. Increased indentation in a Rockwell tester corresponds to a softer material. Despite the use of the same alloy, the reading will be lower.

THE CORRECT ANSWER IS: (A)

540. T851 (in any thickness) is the only heat treatment/temper from among the choices available that meets the 55-ksi requirement.

THE CORRECT ANSWER IS: (D)

PE Practice Exams Published by NCEES

Chemical
Civil: Construction
Civil: Geotechnical
Civil: Structural
Civil: Transportation
Civil: Water Resources and Environmental
Electrical and Computer: Computer Engineering
Electrical and Computer: Electrical and Electronics
Electrical and Computer: Power
Environmental
Mechanical: HVAC and Refrigeration
Mechanical: Thermal and Fluids Systems
Structural Engineering

For more information about these and other NCEES publications and services,
visit NCEES.org or call Client Services at (800) 250-3196.